RECIPES FOR RUNNERS

Sammy Green

W. Foulsham & Co. Ltd.
London • New York • Toronto • Cape Town • Sydney

W. Foulsham & Company Limited
Yeovil Road, Slough, Berkshire, SL1 4JH

ISBN 0–572–01499–6

Copyright © 1991 Sammy Green

Printed in Great Britain at St Edmundsbury Press,
Bury St Edmunds

CONTENTS

INTRODUCTION

Years ago, when I was first bitten by the running bug, my diet was pretty suspect — lots of red meats, cream and sugar. As I began to take running more seriously, meals became an increasing problem. Time was at a premium and the choice of food came to be governed more and more by its effect on bowel habits! Today, little has changed. Runners are still obsessed with their bowels and the excuse I hear most frequently for poor nutrition is lack of time.

Fitting in a proper meal after a training run when your partner's at yoga and your teenage son has eaten the last of the beans, can be a problem and will usually leave you a little low in the energy stakes. The situation invariably degenerates into a mooch round the cupboard and a hasty reheating of anything with an imminent 'sell by' date. For single runners, the picture is even more desperate, with nobody to witness the fact that you haven't eaten a raw carrot since the girlfriend on the macrobiotic diet walked out.

Recent research is beginning to show that, when it comes to running, diet is one of the most important factors affecting performance. Eat a healthy diet and Mother Nature herself will provide you with a major advantage over your rivals without resorting to drugs or tablets.

The following recipes are designed to provide you with extra energy for running without expending too much of it rushing round the kitchen. They are low on salt, sugar, fat and additives but high in carbohydrates, nutrients and fibre. All have been contributed, tried and tested by runners themselves who are already convinced of the benefits of 5-star fuel. And since the amount of evidence linking diet with certain diseases is increasing, following a healthy diet might even ensure you'll live long enough to achieve all those future personal bests!

BREAK THAT FAST

The first meal of the day is by far the most important, especially for runners, and yet it's the meal most likely to be rushed or eliminated altogether. Anyone watching their weight, and that must include the majority of runners, should be aware that one of the surest ways of gaining pounds is to skip breakfast. Yes, you can actually *gain* weight by not eating.

Our basic metabolic rate (BMR) is the rate at which we burn calories. This rate can vary from person to person. The faster your BMR is, the more efficiently your food is metabolised and the less the risk of weight gain. If your BMR is slow, then the metabolic process is lengthened and more calories are laid down as fat. This illustrates why many of us are destined to a life of self-denial, while others indulge with apparent impunity and aren't even runners!

Fortunately, we don't have to sit back piling on the pounds whilst blaming Mother Nature for putting the breaks on our BMR — it is within our power to speed it up. After a night's sleep your rate is at its slowest and eating a wholesome breakfast will immediately send it into top gear. Once you've raised your rate, it will run at the increased speed for up to 15 hours after the activity has finished.

The emphasis in your diet must be on wholefoods because these stimulate the system to work harder, unlike refined white breads and sugar-laden cereals which require hardly any effort at all. So treat yourself to a toaster which will accommodate large brown doorsteps and say goodbye to thin white sliced bread. Only buy muesli without added sugar or mix your own and enjoy it with fresh fruit and yoghurt. If you do resort to commercial cereals, read the labels carefully or you could become a victim of hidden sugar and salt.

Exercise will also stimulate your BMR, which may provide fresh incentive for that early morning run, but do make sure there's time to fill up the fuel tank on your return.

LOADERS' GRANOLA

Makes 10 servings	Metric	Imperial	American
Rolled oats	450 g	1 lb	4 cups
Chopped almonds	50 g	2 oz	½ cup
Wheatgerm	100 g	4 oz	1 cup
Sunflower seeds	50 g	2 oz	½ cup
Desiccated (shredded) coconut	50 g	2 oz	⅔ cup
Chopped stoned (pitted) dates	50 g	2 oz	⅓ cup
Raisins	100 g	4 oz	⅔ cup
Chopped no-need-to-soak dried apricots	50 g	2 oz	⅓ cup
Water	2 tbsp	2 tbsp	2 tbsp
Safflower oil	6 tbsp	6 tbsp	6 tbsp
Vanilla essence	1 tsp	1 tsp	1 tsp

1 Mix together all the dry ingredients, except the dates, raisins and apricots.
2 Mix the water, oil and vanilla and pour over the dry ingredients. Stir well to ensure all the ingredients are evenly coated.
3 Spread the mixture on a large baking tray and cook in a preheated oven at 160°C/325°F (Gas Mark 2) for 45–60 minutes, stirring occasionally to ensure the Granola browns evenly.
4 Remove from the oven and stir in the dried fruits. Leave to cool, then store in an airtight container and use as required.

VARIATION
Although intended as a breakfast cereal, Granola makes a lovely crunchy topping for desserts. If you crave extra sweetness, add a little honey before baking.

CINNAMON AND SULTANA PORRIDGE

This is the ideal breakfast to have after an early-morning run on a frosty day. On your return, put the porridge on to simmer, then by the time you have showered and dried it will be ready and waiting.

Serves 2	Metric	Imperial	American
Pin-head oatmeal	*100 g*	*4 oz*	*⅔ cup*
Water	*600 ml*	*1 pint*	*2½ cups*
Ground cinnamon	*1 tsp*	*1 tsp*	*1 tsp*
Sultanas (golden raisins)	*50 g*	*2 oz*	*⅓ cup*
Plain yoghurt	*2 tbsp*	*2 tbsp*	*2 tbsp*
Clear honey	*2 tsp*	*2 tsp*	*2 tsp*

1 Put the oatmeal in a bowl and pour over the water. Leave to soak overnight.
2 Place the oatmeal and water in a saucepan with the cinnamon and sultanas and bring to the boil. Stir well, then lower the heat and simmer for 20 minutes or until the porridge is thick and creamy. Divide between two bowls.
3 Mix the yoghurt with the honey and place a spoonful on each bowl of steaming porridge.

NOTE
Pin-head oatmeal was used originally for Scots porridge. It has a nuttier flavour than rolled oats. You can vary the ingredients using any dried fruit or nuts.

FRUIT AND NUT MUESLI

Serves 4	Metric	Imperial	American
Barley flakes	4 tbsp	4 tbsp	4 tbsp
Wheat flakes	4 tbsp	4 tbsp	4 tbsp
Rye flakes	4 tbsp	4 tbsp	4 tbsp
Rolled oats	4 tbsp	4 tbsp	4 tbsp
Sesame (benne) seeds	1 tbsp	1 tbsp	1 tbsp
Sunflower seeds	1 tbsp	1 tbsp	1 tbsp
Mixed dried vine fruits	100 g	4 oz	⅔ cup
Chopped no-need-to-soak dried apricots	50 g	2 oz	⅓ cup
Mixed nuts, roughly chopped	100 g	4 oz	¼ lb
Wheatgerm	2 tsp	2 tsp	2 tsp
Grapefruit, peeled and segmented	1	1	1
Orange, peeled and segmented	1	1	1

1 Mix all the dry ingredients and divide between four bowls.
2 Arrange the fresh fruit on top and serve with plain live yoghurt, skimmed milk or fruit juice.

NOTE
Make up a week's supply of the dry mixture and store in an airtight tin. Add fresh fruit just before serving.

OATY OMELETTE

Serves 2	Metric	Imperial	American
Sunflower oil	1 tbsp	1 tbsp	1 tbsp
Large garlic clove, crushed	1	1	1
Small onion, chopped	1	1	1
Mushrooms	100 g	4 oz	1 cup
Medium potato, peeled and diced	1	1	1

Green pepper, deseeded and chopped	½	½	½
Tomatoes, chopped	2	2	2
Large free-range eggs	3	3	3
Skimmed milk	1 tbsp	1 tbsp	1 tbsp
Rolled oats	5 tbsp	5 tbsp	5 tbsp
Paprika, to taste			
Grated Edam cheese	2 tbsp	2 tbsp	2 tbsp

1 Heat the oil in a large frying pan (skillet) and sauté the garlic and all the vegetables, except the tomatoes, for 10–15 minutes or until soft. Add tomatoes and stir.
2 Beat the eggs and stir in the milk, oats and paprika to taste. Pour over the vegetables and cook for 5–10 minutes or until set.
3 Turn on to a heatproof plate, sprinkle with the cheese and place under a preheated grill (broiler) until bubbling. Serve at once.

BREAKFAST CUP

There are many runners who just can't face any solid food first thing in the morning. This liquid meal is one way of ensuring a supply of carbohydrates and other nutrients until such time as the body is more willing to break its fast.

Serves 2	Metric	Imperial	American
Fruit juice	600 ml	1 pint	2½ cups
Wheatgerm	2 tbsp	2 tbsp	2 tbsp
Banana, peeled	1	1	1
Clear honey	2 tbsp	2 tbsp	2 tbsp
Free-range egg	1	1	1
Powdered kelp	1 tsp	1 tsp	1 tsp
Soya flour	50 g	2 oz	½ cup

1 Place all the ingredients in a blender or food processor and blend for 1 minute or until smooth.
2 Pour into two glasses and serve chilled.

HIGH CARBO POTATO SCONES

To save time, peel and grate the potatoes for these tasty scones before you leave for your early-morning run.

Serves 2	Metric	Imperial	American
Potatoes	*1 kg*	*2 lb*	*2 lb*
Plain wholewheat flour	*2 tbsp*	*2 tbsp*	*2 tbsp*
Rolled oats	*2 tbsp*	*2 tbsp*	*2 tbsp*
Onion, finely chopped	*1*	*1*	*1*
Mustard	*1 tsp*	*1 tsp*	*1 tsp*
Free-range eggs	*2*	*2*	*2*
Freshly ground black pepper			
Vegetable oil			

1 Peel the potatoes and grate into a bowl. Leave to stand for 1 hour.
2 Tip the potato into a sieve and press with a wooden spoon to squeeze out all the moisture.
3 Mix the flour, oats, onion and mustard and stir in the potatoes.
4 Beat the eggs and pour on to the mixture. Stir well and season with pepper.
5 Heat a little oil in a frying pan (skillet) and fry tablespoons of the mixture for 3–4 minutes or until golden. Turn and fry the second side for 3–4 minutes. Drain on absorbent kitchen paper and serve with grilled (broiled) tomatoes.

VARIATION
Add a sprinkling of your favourite herbs or chopped chillies to the mixture.

NUTRITION NOTE
The loss of potato peel is more than compensated for by the addition of the oats. Oats are one of the best sources of soluble fibre which means they actually swell in the intestine, thereby delaying the onset of hunger.

THE ENERGY GAP

Do you begin to wilt when the clock strikes four in the afternoon? This is usually the time of day when energy supplies are running low and runners begin to find excuses for missing the evening training session. Those made of sterner stuff use the feeling as an excuse to 'pig out' on cakes, biscuits, cookies and chocolate bars, having convinced themselves that they need instant energy. Unfortunately, by the time the tired feeling overcomes you, it's probably too late to do anything 'instant' about it. All you'll succeed in doing is flooding the system with insulin. The resulting high will be short-lived and the subsequent low worse than the original tiredness.

The fact is that those who experience the energy gap have failed to provide their bodies with sufficient carbohydrate (slow-release energy) to keep them going through the day. What you must do to ensure adequate supplies is to stoke up on bread, potatoes, pasta or fruit. Most runners train after work between six and seven, which means waiting until seven or eight to eat a main meal. Instead of resorting to sugary foods, be prepared and pop a couple of wholewheat sandwiches or even plain wholewheat rolls into your kit bag.

If you've tried this healthy approach and still crave biscuits, etc., I'm afraid you'll have to accept the fact that you've become a sugar addict. As with any other addiction, you'll have to wean yourself slowly away from the empty calorie foods to more wholesome varieties. Firstly, buy your 'fix' from a healthfood shop, where biscuits, etc., tend to be lower in sugar and salt and higher in fibre. Dried fruit mixes are a good choice if you're not slimming but avoid 'trail' mixes containing coconut which is high in saturated fat. The recipes in this section have been included to bridge the gap until such time as you kick the sugar habit. Although many contain sugar, they also contain other nutritious ingredients.

CARROT CAKE

This carrot cake is a favourite recipe of Sandra Harris, a member of the Serpentine Running Club based in London. Although London inspired her to run a 3 hour 35 minute marathon, her native New Zealand introduced her to the pleasures of carrot cake.

Makes 10 slices	Metric	Imperial	American
Plain wholewheat flour	225 g	8 oz	2 cups
Brown sugar	225 g	8 oz	1⅓ cups
Ground cinnamon	2 tsp	2 tsp	2 tsp
Bicarbonate of soda (baking soda)	2 tsp	2 tsp	2 tsp
Large free-range eggs, beaten	3	3	3
Sunflower oil	250 ml	8 fl oz	1 cup
Grated carrot	450 g	1 lb	3 cups

1 Mix the flour, sugar, cinnamon and bicarbonate of soda together.
2 Add the eggs, oil and grated carrot and beat well.
3 Pour into a greased and lined 1 kg (2 lb) loaf tin (pan) and bake in a preheated oven at 190°C/375°F (Gas Mark 5) for 45–60 minutes or until well risen and firm to the touch.
4 Leave to cool slightly in the tin before turning out on to a wire rack.

VARIATION
If you haven't got a weight problem or a conscience, this is scrumptious iced or topped with whipped cream.

DATE AND ORANGE LOAF

Makes 8 slices	Metric	Imperial	American
Chopped stoned (pitted) dates	100 g	4 oz	2/3 cup
Raisins	100 g	4 oz	2/3 cup
Brown sugar	100 g	4 oz	2/3 cup
Water	120 ml	4 fl oz	1/2 cup
Grated rind and juice of 1 orange			
Vegetable margarine	75 g	3 oz	1/3 cup
Free-range egg, beaten	1	1	1
Plain wholewheat flour	225 g	8 oz	2 cups
Baking powder	2 tsp	2 tsp	2 tsp

1 Put the fruit and sugar in a saucepan, add the water and bring to the boil. Remove from the heat and add the orange juice and rind. Stir in the margarine, egg, flour and baking powder.
2 Beat well and pour into a greased and lined 450 g (1 lb) loaf tin (pan) and bake in a preheated oven at 180°C/350°F (Gas Mark 4) for about 1 hour or until risen and firm to the touch.

NUTRITION NOTE
If you're low on B vitamins and potassium, and need those extra carbohydrates, a slice of this cake will help.

WALNUT AND BANANA BREAD

Makes 8 slices	Metric	Imperial	American
Vegetable margarine	*50 g*	*2 oz*	*¼ cup*
Brown sugar	*75 g*	*3 oz*	*½ cup*
Free-range eggs	*3*	*3*	*3*
Large bananas, peeled and mashed	*3*	*3*	*3*
Self-raising wholewheat flour	*225 g*	*8 oz*	*2 cups*
Chopped walnuts	*175 g*	*6 oz*	*1½ cups*

1 Cream the margarine and sugar together until light and fluffy. Beat in the eggs, one at a time, beating well after each addition until the mixture is smooth.
2 Beat in the mashed bananas, then stir in the flour and walnuts.
3 Pour the mixture into a greased and lined 450 g (1 lb) loaf tin (pan) and bake in a preheated oven at 180°C/350°F (Gas Mark 4) for 55 minutes or until risen and firm to the touch.

NUTRITION NOTE
Walnuts are a good source of linoleic acid, essential for the utilization of fats.

PINEAPPLE AND SULTANA LOAF

Makes 8 slices	Metric	Imperial	American
Vegetable margarine	100 g	4 oz	½ cup
Brown sugar	100 g	4 oz	⅔ cup
Free-range eggs, beaten	2	2	2
Plain wholewheat flour	225 g	8 oz	2 cups
Baking powder	2 tsp	2 tsp	2 tsp
Sultanas (golden raisins)	25 g	1 oz	3 tbsp
Chopped walnuts	25 g	1 oz	¼ cup
Small can of crushed pineapple, no added sugar	1	1	1

1 Cream the margarine and sugar together until light and fluffy. Beat in the eggs, a little at a time, beating well after each addition.
2 Fold in the flour and baking powder, then stir in the sultanas, walnuts, crushed pineapple and pineapple juice. Mix well.
3 Pour the mixture into a greased and lined 450 g (1 lb) loaf tin (pan) and bake in a preheated oven at 180°C/350°F (Gas Mark 4) for about 1 hour or until risen and firm to the touch.

VARIATION
The fruit combinations can be varied in this moist loaf. Prunes and rhubarb produce a version particularly high in carbohydrates.

BRAN LOAF

This deliciously simple high-fibre loaf was contributed by Mrs. Lynne Kirk who lives in Leeds. She describes herself as a 'keen jogger married to a serious runner'. Both she and her husband have developed a taste for healthier food since becoming aware of the benefits of exercise.

Any dried fruit can be used for the loaf but stoned (pitted) dates are particularly good. Add your favourite spices and seeds for variety and keep the loaf for at least a day before slicing.

Makes 8 slices

	Metric	Imperial	American
Bran	100 g	4 oz	1 cup
Soft brown sugar	75 g	3 oz	½ cup
Mixed dried fruit	175 g	6 oz	1 cup
Skimmed milk	250 ml	8 fl oz	1 cup
Self-raising wholewheat flour	100 g	4 oz	1 cup

1 Place all the ingredients, except the flour, in a bowl and leave to stand for 1 hour.
2 Add the flour and stir lightly, then place in a greased and lined 450 g (1 lb) loaf tin (pan) and bake in a preheated oven at 220°C/425°F (Gas Mark 7) for 15 minutes. Reduce the heat to 180°C/350°F (Gas Mark 4) and continue cooking for a further 45 minutes.
3 Leave to cool in the tin before storing in an airtight container.
4 Slice and spread with a low-cholesterol margarine.

CINNAMON COOKIES

Allen Bennet, a keen marathoner from Kirby, enjoys the crunchiness of these spicy biscuits. The brown rice provides extra carbohydrate and fibre.

Makes 30	Metric	Imperial	American
Plain wholewheat flour	*450 g*	*1 lb*	*4 cups*
Cooked brown rice	*350 g*	*12 oz*	*2 cups*
Ground cinnamon	*1 tsp*	*1 tsp*	*1 tsp*
Apple juice concentrate	*120 ml*	*4 fl oz*	*½ cup*
Corn oil	*120 ml*	*4 fl oz*	*½ cup*
Vanilla essence	*1 tsp*	*1 tsp*	*1 tsp*

1 Put all the dry ingredients in a bowl and mix well.
   Combine the apple juice concentrate with the oil and
   vanilla, pour on to the flour mixture and mix well. Add
   sufficient water to produce a dropping consistency.
2 Drop spoonfuls of the mixture on to a greased baking
   sheet and bake in a preheated oven at 180°C/350°F (Gas
   Mark 4) for 30 minutes.

HIGH ENERGY CHEWS

Annette Sheffield, from Derby, has been running for many
years and always keeps a supply of these delicious chews in
her kit bag. They're a healthier source of instant energy than
commercial sweets. Treat yourself to one *after* a race or training run rather than before.

Makes 12–15	Metric	Imperial	American
Blanched almonds	*50 g*	*2 oz*	*½ cup*
Sunflower seeds	*50 g*	*2 oz*	*½ cup*
Stoned (pitted) dates	*50 g*	*2 oz*	*½ cup*
Raisins	*50 g*	*2 oz*	*⅓ cup*
No-need-to-soak dried apricots	*50 g*	*2 oz*	*½ cup*
Desiccated (shredded) coconut	*50 g*	*2 oz*	*⅔ cup*

1 Put the almonds and sunflower seeds in a blender or
   food processor and grind. Add the dried fruits and
   process for a further 2–3 minutes.
2 Form the mixture into small balls and roll in the coconut.

SUNFLOWER AND APPLE SCONES

Makes 12	Metric	Imperial	American
Self-raising wholewheat flour	450 g	1 lb	4 cups
Vegetable margarine	175 g	6 oz	¾ cup
Sunflower seeds	50 g	2 oz	½ cup
Eating apple, peeled, cored and grated	100 g	4 oz	¼ lb
Sultanas (golden raisins)	100 g	4 oz	⅔ cup
Skimmed milk	250 ml	8 fl oz	1 cup
Plain yoghurt	2 tbsp	2 tbsp	2 tbsp

1 Place the flour in a bowl and rub (cut) in the margarine until the mixture resembles breadcrumbs. Stir in the sunflower seeds, apple and sultanas.
2 Make a well in the centre of the mixture and pour in the milk and yoghurt. Mix lightly to form a soft dough.
3 Turn the dough on to a floured surface and knead lightly, then roll out to a round 2.5 cm/1 inch thick. Using a 5 cm/2 inch pastry cutter, cut out 12 scones and place them on a greased baking sheet.
4 Bake the scones in a preheated oven at 220°C/425°F (Gas Mark 7) for 15 minutes or until well risen. Serve plain or with a sugar-free jam.

NUTRITION NOTE
Sunflower seeds are a good source of fatty acids which are essential for the burning of saturated fat.

CARBOHYDRATES — A LOADED QUESTION

A great deal of time and a fair amount of energy has gone into the widespread belief that the pre-race meal is all-important. Many a runner, who lives on high-protein meals all year, has feasted the night before a race, expecting, like Eros, to sprout wings on his or her feet by morning.

Carbohydrates should be the staple food of all runners but not only on pre-race night. To maximize your performance, the most important factor is consistent training, and to enable you to accomplish this the body requires a continuous supply of energy. Sorry, I know cakes, biscuits and sweets are full of carbohydrates, but the energy they produce is instant and short-lived. These are known as 'simple' carbohydrates and they'll let you down in the 'long run'!

'Complex' carbohydrates are what we need and they are found predominantly in potatoes, bread, cereals and grains. This food group should make up at least 55 per cent of your diet, which is good news on the economic front because they're comparatively cheap foods. Runners on high-carbo diets will be able to afford more pairs of running shoes!

The technique known as 'carbo-loading' has been modified over the years and has now emerged as a very simple routine. Basically, it requires the consumption of a larger proportion of carbohydrates (say 70 per cent) 3–4 days before an endurance event, combined with a reduction in training mileage. This extra carbo is then converted to glycogen and stored in the liver ready to be utilized by the runner. Unfortunately, we're only talking about improvements of minutes so don't expect miracles.

One of the most important times for 'carbo-loading' is often overlooked, that is the post-race situation. When your glycogen stores are depleted you're in danger of grinding to a halt or risking injury when you resume training with a low fuel tank. Keep those stores topped up with the following recipes designed to take the boredom out of 'loading'.

PASTA WITH MANDARINS AND PRAWNS

Serves 4	Metric	Imperial	American
Wholewheat pasta shells	350 g	12 oz	3 cups
Olive oil	2 tbsp	2 tbsp	2 tbsp
Egg yolk	1	1	1
Grated rind and juice of 1 lemon			
Mandarin oranges, peeled and segmented	4	4	4
Cooked peeled prawns (shrimp)	100 g	4 oz	½ cup
Grated Parmesan cheese	100 g	4 oz	⅔ cup
Sesame (benne) seeds	1 tbsp	1 tbsp	1 tbsp
Chopped fresh parsley	2 tbsp	2 tbsp	2 tbsp

1 Cook the pasta shells in plenty of boiling water, with 1 tsp olive oil added, for 8–10 minutes or until tender.
2 Meanwhile, mix the egg yolk, lemon rind and lemon juice.
3 Drain the pasta shells and place in a warmed serving bowl. Stir in the remaining olive oil, the mandarin segments and prawns.
4 Pour over the egg and lemon mixture and sprinkle with the Parmesan, sesame seeds and parsley. Toss well and serve at once.

NUTRITION NOTE
It's an interesting fact that parsley actually contains more vitamin C than oranges. So if it's winter colds that bug you, this pasta should help to build up your resistance.

TUNA TWISTS

This dish takes only about 15 minutes to prepare and cook and is the invention of a marathon runner who is just as speedy on the road as she is in the kitchen. Debbie Heath runs for London Olympiads and has a weekly training average of 60 miles. She has produced a 2 hour 45 minute marathon and a 58 minute 10-miler, but I'm not sure if it was the tuna pasta that helped or the fact that she's an accountant. There's no doubt she's certainly figured it out!

Serves 3–4	Metric	Imperial	American
Wholewheat pasta twists	350 g	12 oz	3 cups
Olive oil	1 tsp	1 tsp	1 tsp
Vegetable margarine	25 g	1 oz	2 tbsp
Large onion, sliced	1	1	1
Mushrooms, sliced	100 g	4 oz	1 cup
Small can of tuna, drained	1	1	1
400 g/14 oz can red kidney beans, drained	1	1	1
Grated cheese	100 g	4 oz	1 cup

1 Cook the pasta in plenty of boiling water, with the olive oil added, for 8–10 minutes or until tender.
2 Meanwhile, melt the margarine in a large frying pan (skillet) or wok and lightly fry the onion for about 5 minutes or until soft. Add the mushrooms and stir-fry for a further 2–3 minutes.
3 Stir the tuna and kidney beans into the onion and mushrooms and continue to cook for 5 minutes.
4 Drain the pasta and add to the frying pan, stirring well. Remove from the heat and stir in the grated cheese. Serve immediately with a large mixed salad.

CHICKEN LASAGNE

Serves 4	Metric	Imperial	American
Sunflower oil	2 tbsp	2 tbsp	2 tbsp
Large onion, chopped	1	1	1
Red pepper, deseeded and sliced	1	1	1
Mushrooms, sliced	100 g	4 oz	1 cup
Garlic cloves, crushed	2	2	2
Dried oregano	1 tsp	1 tsp	1 tsp
Plain wholewheat flour	40 g	1½ oz	6 tbsp
Mustard powder	1 tsp	1 tsp	1 tsp
Soya milk	450 ml	¾ pint	2 cups
Chicken stock (bouillon) cube	1	1	1
Diced cooked chicken	300 g	10 oz	1⅔ cups
Chopped walnuts	100 g	4 oz	1 cup
Grated Parmesan cheese	75 g	3 oz	¾ cup
Sheets of pre-cooked wholewheat lasagne	12	12	12
Paprika	1 tsp	1 tsp	1 tsp

1 Heat the oil in a large saucepan and sauté the onion and pepper for 5–10 minutes or until soft. Add the mushrooms, garlic and oregano and cook for a further 2 minutes.
2 Stir in the flour and mustard and cook for 2 minutes over a low heat. Remove from the heat and gradually add the milk, beating constantly. Crumble in the stock cube and cook, stirring, until the sauce thickens.
3 Stir the chicken, walnuts and 50 g/2 oz/½ cup Parmesan into the sauce and cook until heated through.
4 Place four sheets of lasagne in the base of an ovenproof dish and pour over one third of the sauce. Cover with another four sheets of lasagne and half the remaining sauce, then add another layer of lasagne and finish with the remaining sauce.
5 Sprinkle with the remaining Parmesan cheese and the paprika and bake in a preheated oven at 200°C/400°F (Gas Mark 6) for 30 minutes or until bubbling and browned. Serve with a large salad.

CHICKEN AND CHESTNUT PASTA

Martin Avery picked up this oriental pasta recipe whilst training in the Far East. As his mileage was restricted by the heat he spent time working out in the kitchen. He says this spaghetti dish is equally tempting served with noodles.

Serves 4	Metric	Imperial	American
Wholewheat spaghetti	*450 g*	*1 lb*	*1 lb*
Olive oil	*1 tsp*	*1 tsp*	*1 tsp*
Cooked chicken, skinned	*225– 350 g*	*8–12 oz*	*½–¾ lb*
Sesame (benne) oil	*2 tbsp*	*2 tbsp*	*2 tbsp*
Garlic cloves, crushed	*4*	*4*	*4*
Peeled and grated fresh root ginger	*2 tsp*	*2 tsp*	*2 tsp*
Wine vinegar	*2 tbsp*	*2 tbsp*	*2 tbsp*
Tamari or soya sauce	*1 tbsp*	*1 tbsp*	*1 tbsp*
Peanut butter	*100 g*	*4 oz*	*½ cup*
Red raisins	*50 g*	*2 oz*	*⅓ cup*
Sliced water chestnuts	*50 g*	*2 oz*	*½ cup*

1 Cook the spaghetti in plenty of boiling water, with the olive oil added, for 8–10 minutes or until tender.
2 Meanwhile, cut the chicken into thin strips about 2.5 cm/1 inch long.
3 Heat the sesame oil in a large frying pan (skillet) or wok and quickly stir-fry the garlic and ginger. Stir in the vinegar, tamari and peanut butter to make a sauce. If it's too thick, dilute with stock or water.
4 Add the raisins, water chestnuts and chicken and continue cooking until heated through.
5 Drain the pasta and pour over the sauce. Serve with a salad of diced cucumber, sweetcorn and tomato.

PETER'S SPINACH AND BROCCOLI PASTA

Peter is the marathon-running proprietor of Peter's Restaurant in Swiss Cottage, North London. A chef by trade, he now spends his time devising healthy recipes for his fit customers. He has obviously included kelp in this recipe to ensure a good supply of iodine, essential for regulating metabolism. Researchers fed racehorses with extra iodine and produced an increase in speed and stamina.

Serves 4	Metric	Imperial	American
Sunflower oil	2 tbsp	2 tbsp	2 tbsp
Garlic cloves, crushed	2	2	2
Onions, chopped	2	2	2
Peeled and grated fresh root ginger	1 tsp	1 tsp	1 tsp
Medium leeks, sliced	3	3	3
Wholewheat pasta (penne, shells, etc.)	350 g	12 oz	3 cups
Olive oil	3 tsp	3 tsp	3 tsp
Broccoli, cut into florets	450 g	1 lb	1 lb
Spinach, chopped	225 g	8 oz	½ lb
Powdered kelp	1 tsp	1 tsp	1 tsp
Dried basil	1 tsp	1 tsp	1 tsp
Tamari	1 tsp	1 tsp	1 tsp

1 Heat the sunflower oil in a large frying pan (skillet) or wok and sauté the garlic and onions for 5–10 minutes or until transparent. Add the ginger and leeks, cover with a lid and sweat the vegetables for 10–15 minutes.
2 Meanwhile, cook the pasta in boiling water, with 1 tsp olive oil added, for 8–10 minutes or until tender.
3 Remove the lid of the pan and place the broccoli on top of the leeks and onions. Finally, place the spinach on top and replace the lid. Continue to sweat for about 8 minutes or until the broccoli is cooked.
4 Drain the pasta and add to the pan with the kelp, basil and tamari. Stir well and dress with a little olive oil.

SPICED TAGLIATELLE

To save time, prepare the sauce for this tasty pasta dish before running. That way the flavours can develop and all you have to do on your return is cook the pasta whilst taking your après-run shower!

Serves 4	Metric	Imperial	American
Vegetable oil	*50 ml*	*2 fl oz*	*¼ cup*
Large onion, chopped	*1*	*1*	*1*
Green pepper, deseeded and chopped	*1*	*1*	*1*
Small green chilli, chopped	*1*	*1*	*1*
Garlic cloves, crushed	*2*	*2*	*2*
400 g/14 oz can tomatoes	*1*	*1*	*1*
Raisins	*50 g*	*2 oz*	*⅓ cup*
Flaked (slivered) almonds	*100 g*	*4 oz*	*1 cup*
Dried basil	*1 tsp*	*1 tsp*	*1 tsp*
Dried oregano	*1 tsp*	*1 tsp*	*1 tsp*
Wholewheat or spinach tagliatelle	*350 g*	*12 oz*	*3 cups*
Grated Parmesan cheese, to serve	*50 g*	*2 oz*	*½ cup*

1 Heat the oil in a large saucepan and sauté the onion, green pepper, chilli and garlic for 5–10 minutes or until soft.
2 Add the tomatoes and their juice, the raisins, almonds and herbs. Simmer for 10–15 minutes or until the sauce thickens.
3 Meanwhile, cook the pasta in plenty of boiling water, with 1 tsp oil added, for 8–10 minutes or until tender.
4 Drain and serve with the sauce and Parmesan cheese.

TODAY'S RUNNER LASAGNE

This *Today's Runner* recipe comes from Assistant Editor Fionn Lawlor, herself a keen runner. She claims this lasagne is equally good using courgettes (zucchini) for those who don't like mushrooms.

Serves 4	Metric	Imperial	American
Vegetable oil	3 tbsp	3 tbsp	3 tbsp
Onion, chopped	1	1	1
Red pepper, deseeded and chopped	1	1	1
Green pepper, deseeded and chopped	1	1	1
Garlic cloves, crushed	2	2	2
Mixed dried herbs	1 tsp	1 tsp	1 tsp
Tomato purée (paste), to taste			
400 g/14 oz can tomatoes	1	1	1
Mushrooms	225 g	8 oz	½ lb
Canned tuna	350 g	12 oz	¾ lb
Skimmed milk	300 ml	½ pint	1¼ cups
Cornflour (cornstarch)	25 g	1 oz	¼ cup
Grated cheese	100 g	4 oz	1 cup
Sheets of pre-cooked wholewheat lasagne	12	12	12
Grated Parmesan cheese			

1 Heat 2 tbsp oil in a large frying pan (skillet) or wok and sauté the onion, peppers and garlic for 5–10 minutes or until soft. Stir in the mixed herbs.
2 Add the tomato purée and can of tomatoes with their juice and simmer gently for 10 minutes.
3 Fry the mushrooms separately in the remaining oil for about 10 minutes or until crisp. Stir in the tuna.
4 Bring the milk to the boil in a small saucepan. Mix the cornflour to a paste with a little water and stir into the milk. Add the grated cheese and stir until it melts.
5 Place half the vegetable mixture in the base of a greased ovenproof dish and cover with a layer of lasagne. Spoon in another layer of vegetables, then add another layer of

lasagne and top with half the cheese sauce. Follow with more lasagne, and a layer of tuna and mushrooms. Finally, pour on the remaining cheese sauce.

6 Top the lasagne with grated Parmesan cheese and bake in a preheated oven at 190°C/375°F (Gas Mark 5) for 45 minutes or until brown and bubbling.

PASTA WITH MUSHROOM AND TOMATO SAUCE

Serves 4	Metric	Imperial	American
Wholewheat pasta shapes	350 g	12 oz	3 cups
Olive oil	2 tbsp	2 tbsp	2 tbsp
Onion, chopped	1	1	1
Garlic cloves, crushed	2	2	2
Button mushrooms	100 g	4 oz	1 cup
Dried basil	2 tsp	2 tsp	2 tsp
Dried oregano	2 tsp	2 tsp	2 tsp
400 g/14 oz can tomatoes	1	1	1
Tomato purée (paste)	5 tbsp	5 tbsp	5 tbsp
Freshly ground black pepper			
Grated Parmesan cheese	50 g	2 oz	½ cup

1 Cook the pasta in plenty of boiling water, with 1 tsp olive oil added, for 8–10 minutes or until just tender.

2 Meanwhile, heat the remaining olive oil in a large frying pan (skillet) or wok and stir-fry the onion for about 5 minutes or until transparent. Stir in the garlic and cook for a further 2 minutes.

3 Add the mushrooms, herbs, tomatoes with their juice and tomato purée. Season to taste with black pepper, stir well and heat through gently, without boiling. Drain the pasta and divide between four warmed serving plates.

4 Pour the sauce over the pasta, sprinkle with Parmesan cheese and serve at once.

QUILTER'S PASTA

David Quilter is an actor and does most of his running for the
TV Times Team raising money for Leukaemia research. He's
still chasing a sub-3 hour marathon and hopefully a few
bowls of his tasty pasta will help him along the way.

Serves 2	Metric	Imperial	American
Wholewheat pasta shells	225 g	8 oz	2 cups
Olive oil	2 tbsp	2 tbsp	2 tbsp
Large onions, sliced	4	4	4
Small green pepper, deseeded and sliced	1	1	1
Large flat mushrooms, sliced	225 g	8 oz	½ lb
Dried herbs (see Note)	1 tsp	1 tsp	1 tsp
Garlic cloves, crushed (optional)	2	2	2
Soya sauce, to taste (see Note)			
Freshly ground black pepper			

1 Cook the pasta in plenty of boiling water, with 1 tsp
  olive oil added, for 8–10 minutes or until tender.
2 Meanwhile, heat the remaining oil in a large frying pan
  (skillet) or wok and stir-fry the onions for about 5
  minutes or until just turning limp. Add the green pepper
  and continue to stir-fry until the onions are beginning to
  brown.
3 Add the mushrooms, herbs and garlic, if used, and
  stir-fry for a further 2 minutes. Stir in the soya sauce and
  season with black pepper.
4 Drain the pasta and stir into the vegetables. Mix well
  before turning into a warmed serving dish.

NOTE
The flavours of this pasta dish can be varied according to
the amount of soya sauce you use. David Quilter
recommends using plenty! As for the dried herbs — choose
whichever are your favourites.

COLIN'S EXTRA SPECIAL

Bill Glad runs for Windsor, Slough and Eton although he hails originally from America. This delicious dish helped him on his way to a 2 hour 17 minute marathon. The recipe was devised by Bill's running partner, Colin — hence the title!

Serves 2–3 (or one runner on 100 miles per week!)	Metric	Imperial	American
Spinach, washed and drained	175 g	6 oz	6 oz
Vegetable margarine	25 g	1 oz	2 tbsp
Medium leek, chopped	1	1	1
Medium onion, chopped	1	1	1
Chopped mushrooms	175 g	6 oz	1½ cups
Wholewheat pasta shapes, cooked	175 g	6 oz	1½ cups
Stoned (pitted) green olives, chopped	5–6	5–6	5–6
Jar of bolognese sauce	½	½	½
Cooked chopped bacon (optional)	175 g	6 oz	¾ cup
Free-range egg	1	1	1
Grated Jarlsberg cheese	175 g	6 oz	1½ cups
Dried herbs, to taste			

1 Place the spinach in a large saucepan with only the water clinging to its leaves from washing. Cover and cook over a medium heat until just beginning to shrink.
2 Meanwhile, melt the margarine in the biggest frying pan (skillet) or wok you can find (this dish has a tendency to grow) and sauté the leek and onion for 5–10 minutes or until soft. Add the mushrooms and stir-fry for a further minute.
3 Drain the spinach and stir into the fried vegetables with the pasta shapes. Add the olives, bolognese sauce, bacon, if used, and the egg, and mix well.
4 Finally, add the cheese and herbs. Continue to cook, stirring, until the cheese melts and the eggs begin to set. Serve at once.

VEGETABLE AND PEANUT BOLOGNESE

Serves 4	Metric	Imperial	American
Wholewheat spaghetti	225 g	8 oz	½ lb
Sunflower oil	2 tbsp	2 tbsp	2 tbsp
Onions, chopped	2	2	2
Large garlic clove, crushed	1	1	1
Courgettes (zucchini), sliced	450 g	1 lb	1 lb
Green pepper, deseeded and diced	1	1	1
Mushrooms, sliced	100 g	4 oz	1 cup
Dried basil	1 tsp	1 tsp	1 tsp
Dried oregano	1 tsp	1 tsp	1 tsp
Unsalted peanuts	175 g	6 oz	1 cup
Tomato purée (paste)	2 tbsp	2 tbsp	2 tbsp
400 g/14 oz can tomatoes	1	1	1
Freshly ground black pepper			
Grated Parmesan cheese, to serve			

1 Cook the spaghetti in plenty of boiling water, with 1 tsp oil added, for 8–10 minutes or until tender.
2 Meanwhile, heat the remaining oil in a large frying pan (skillet) or wok and sauté the onions for about 5 minutes or until soft.
3 Add the garlic, courgettes and green pepper and stir-fry for about 5 minutes or until the courgettes are almost cooked. Stir in the mushrooms and continue cooking for a further 2–3 minutes. Add the herbs and peanuts, stirring continuously.
4 Mix the tomato purée and canned tomatoes together and add to the pan. Simmer gently until the vegetables are just soft and heated through. Season to taste with pepper.
5 Drain the pasta and arrange on serving plates. Spoon the bolognese on top and serve with Parmesan cheese.

AUBERGINE AND WALNUT NOODLES

Serves 4	Metric	Imperial	American
Pasta noodles	*225 g*	*8 oz*	*2 cups*
Olive oil	*2 tbsp*	*2 tbsp*	*2 tbsp*
Large onion, chopped	*1*	*1*	*1*
Large aubergine (eggplant),			
* cubed*	*1*	*1*	*1*
Large garlic clove, crushed	*1*	*1*	*1*
Chopped walnuts	*50 g*	*2 oz*	*½ cup*
Sesame (benne) seeds	*1 tbsp*	*1 tbsp*	*1 tbsp*
French (Dijon) mustard	*2 tsp*	*2 tsp*	*2 tsp*
Red wine vinegar	*1 tbsp*	*1 tbsp*	*1 tbsp*
Tamari	*1 tbsp*	*1 tbsp*	*1 tbsp*
Chopped fresh coriander	*3 tbsp*	*3 tbsp*	*3 tbsp*
* or dried coriander*	*1 tbsp*	*1 tbsp*	*1 tbsp*
Water	*2 tbsp*	*2 tbsp*	*2 tbsp*

1 Cook the noodles in plenty of boiling water, with 1 tsp oil added, for 8–10 minutes or until tender.
2 Meanwhile, heat the remaining olive oil in a frying pan (skillet) or wok and sauté the onion for about 5 minutes or until transparent. Add the aubergine and garlic and stir-fry over a very high heat for about 10 minutes or until soft.
3 Stir in the walnuts and sesame seeds and cook for a further 2–3 minutes.
4 Mix together the mustard, vinegar, tamari, coriander and water. Pour over the aubergine mixture and simmer gently until the sauce has thickened.
5 Drain the noodles, place in a large warmed serving dish and pour over the aubergine sauce. Serve with a tomato salad.

VARIATION
Carnivores can add any chopped leftover chicken or meat to the sauce, if liked.

BARLEY AND MUSHROOM PILAFF

Serves 4	Metric	Imperial	American
Vegetable margarine	100 g	4 oz.	½ cup
Large onions, chopped	2	2	2
Garlic cloves, crushed	2	2	2
Pot barley	450 g	1 lb	1 lb
Mushrooms, sliced	225 g	8 oz	2 cups
Raisins	100 g	4 oz	⅔ cup
Large tomatoes, chopped	4	4	4
Boiling vegetable stock	750 ml	1¼ pints	3 cups
Chopped fresh parsley	2 tbsp	2 tbsp	2 tbsp
Freshly ground black pepper			

1 Melt the margarine in a large saucepan and sauté the onions and garlic for about 5 minutes or until soft.
2 Add the barley and stir-fry for 2–3 minutes or until golden. Stir in the mushrooms, raisins and tomatoes and continue to cook for a further 2–3 minutes.
3 Pour in half the stock and either simmer gently in the pan for 30 minutes or transfer to a casserole and cook in a preheated oven at 180°C/350°F (Gas Mark 4).
4 Pour in the remaining stock and continue cooking for a further 30 minutes or until all the liquid has been absorbed and the grains are cooked.
5 Stir in the parsley and season to taste with black pepper. Serve as an alternative to potatoes or rice.

VARIATION
To transform this into a main dish you can stir in any leftover vegetables, chicken, meat, fish, nuts or beans.

NUTRITION NOTE
All runners should eat whole grains regularly to obtain a full complement of B vitamins. Remember, because the B group of vitamins are water soluble, they need replenishing every day.

MUSHROOMS WITH MILLET

Serves 4	Metric	Imperial	American
Millet	350 g	12 oz	¾ lb
Sunflower oil	2 tbsp	2 tbsp	2 tbsp
Onions, sliced	2	2	2
Garlic cloves, crushed	2	2	2
Mushrooms, sliced	450 g	1 lb	1 lb
Tomatoes, chopped	225 g	8 oz	½ lb
Cooked green lentils or cooked chicken, diced	225 g	8 oz	½ lb
Chopped fresh mint	2 tbsp	2 tbsp	2 tbsp
Freshly ground black pepper			
Paprika	1 tbsp	1 tbsp	1 tbsp
Hard-boiled (hard-cooked) eggs, sliced	2	2	2

1 Cook the millet in boiling water for 20 minutes or until tender. Drain well.
2 Meanwhile, heat the oil in a frying pan (skillet) and sauté the onions for about 5 minutes or until transparent. Add the garlic, mushrooms and tomatoes and continue to cook for a further 2 minutes. Stir in the cooked lentils or chicken and the drained millet.
3 Transfer the mixture to a serving dish and fork in the mint and pepper to taste. Sprinkle with paprika and garnish with sliced hard-boiled eggs.

NUTRITION NOTE
Millet is certainly not just food for the birds. It contains almost three times as much carbohydrate as brown rice, all the amino acids and is high in thiamin, riboflavin and many minerals. So if you want to fly like a bird, start eating millet!

GREAT GRAINS AND BEANS

Serves 4	Metric	Imperial	American
Wheat grains, soaked overnight	100 g	4 oz	1 cup
Brown long grain rice	100 g	4 oz	½ cup
Sunflower oil	3 tbsp	3 tbsp	3 tbsp
Onions, chopped	2	2	2
Garlic cloves, crushed	3	3	3
Medium potatoes, scrubbed and diced	2	2	2
Ground coriander	1 tsp	1 tsp	1 tsp
Cumin seeds	1 tsp	1 tsp	1 tsp
Ground turmeric	1 tsp	1 tsp	1 tsp
Chilli powder, to taste			
Cooked mung beans	225 g	8 oz	¾ cup
Tomato purée (paste)	1 tbsp	1 tbsp	1 tbsp
Water	150 ml	¼ pint	⅔ cup
Chopped no-need-to-soak dried apricots	50 g	2 oz	⅓ cup
Flaked (slivered) almonds	50 g	2 oz	½ cup
Tomatoes, sliced	4	4	4

1 Cook the wheat and rice separately in boiling water until tender. The wheat will take about 1 hour and the rice about 30 minutes.
2 Meanwhile, heat the oil in a large frying pan (skillet) or wok and sauté the ooions for about 5 minutes or until transparent. Add the garlic and potato and continue to cook for a further 5 minutes. Stir in the spices and beans, lower the heat and cook for 5 minutes more.
3 Mix the tomato purée with the water and pour into the vegetable mixture with the apricots. Continue to simmer until the potato is tender and the tomato juice almost absorbed. Meanwhile, drain the rice and wheat.
4 Stir the almonds, rice and wheat into the pan, and cook until heated through. Garnish with sliced tomatoes and serve with salad.

TUNA RISOTTO

This must be one of the fastest meals around. I can run with my husband, then shower and have the risotto on the table almost before he's had time to calculate the mileage! The rice can be cooked in advance.

Serves 4	Metric	Imperial	American
Sunflower oil	2 tbsp	2 tbsp	2 tbsp
Onions, sliced	2	2	2
Garlic cloves, crushed	2	2	2
Green pepper, deseeded and sliced	1	1	1
Celery stalks, sliced	2	2	2
Cooked peas	100 g	4 oz	¾ cup
Mushrooms, sliced	100 g	4 oz	1 cup
Dried sage	1 tsp	1 tsp	1 tsp
Canned tuna, drained and flaked	400 g	14 oz	14 oz
Cooked brown rice	450 g	1 lb	1 lb
Freshly ground black pepper			

1 Heat the oil in a large frying pan (skillet) or wok. Add all the vegetables, except the peas and mushrooms, and stir-fry for 10 minutes.
2 Stir in the sage and finally the tuna, rice, peas and mushrooms.
3 Cook until the risotto is piping hot, then remove from the heat, season to taste with black pepper and serve with a large salad.

VARIATION
Vegetarians can substitute 100–175 g/4–6 oz/1–1½ cups cashew nuts for the tuna.

RICE AND COURGETTE HASH

You can prepare the grain and vegetable part of this dish well before you plan to run. Store, covered, in a cool place, then all you have to do is pour over the topping and take a shower while it bakes.

Serves 4	Metric	Imperial	American
Sunflower oil	2 tbsp	2 tbsp	2 tbsp
Medium onions, sliced	2	2	2
Medium courgettes (zucchini), sliced	3	3	3
Medium peppers, deseeded and sliced	3	3	3
Tamari	2 tsp	2 tsp	2 tsp
Paprika	1 tsp	1 tsp	1 tsp
Cooked mixed grains or brown rice	450 g	1 lb	1 lb
400 g/14 oz can tomatoes	1	1	1
Free-range eggs	2	2	2
Plain yoghurt	300 ml	½ pint	1¼ cups

1 Heat the oil in a large frying pan (skillet) or wok and stir-fry the onions, courgettes and peppers for 5–10 minutes or until soft. Stir in the tamari and paprika and cook for a further 2 minutes.
2 Place a layer of grains or rice in a greased casserole and spoon over half the vegetables.
3 Drain the can of tomatoes, reserving the juice, and cut the tomatoes into slices. Arrange some of the slices over the vegetables. Continue to layer the ingredients in this way, ending with a layer of grains. Pour over the reserved tomato juice.
4 Beat the eggs and yoghurt together and pour over the top of the hash. Bake in a preheated oven at 190°C/375°F (Gas Mark 5) for 20–30 minutes or until the top is golden and set. Serve with fresh green vegetables.

PIQUANT POLENTA

Serves 4	Metric	Imperial	American
Hot water	*1 litre*	*2 pints*	*5 cups*
Coarse cornmeal (maizemeal or polenta)	*225 g*	*8 oz*	*1½ cups*
Vegetable margarine	*50 g*	*2 oz*	*¼ cup*
Small onion, chopped	*1*	*1*	*1*
Small green pepper, deseeded and chopped	*1*	*1*	*1*
Small red pepper, deseeded and chopped	*1*	*1*	*1*
Chopped dried chillies	*1 tsp*	*1 tsp*	*1 tsp*
Free-range egg, beaten	*1*	*1*	*1*
Cornmeal, for coating	*50 g*	*2 oz*	*½ cup*
Freshly ground black pepper			

1 Pour the hot water into a saucepan and sprinkle on the cornmeal. Stir in the margarine and cook for 5–10 minutes or until the mixture thickens. Remove from the heat and beat in the onion, peppers and chillies.
2 Press the mixture into the bottom of a greased 18 × 27 cm/7 × 11 inch baking tray and leave in the refrigerator until set.
3 Turn the polenta out of the baking tray and cut into 16 pieces. Brush with beaten egg and coat with cornmeal.
4 Deep fry until golden brown, sprinkle with black pepper to taste and serve hot with a tomato or chilli sauce and a green salad.

NUTRITION NOTE
Although maizemeal contains less protein than other cereals it is still a useful source of carbohydrate and vitamin A. It makes a pleasant change from potatoes and pasta in the runner's diet. Coeliacs should find a place for its use as it contains no gluten.

ONE-POT BARLEY STEW

Serves 4	Metric	Imperial	American
Vegetable oil	2 tbsp	2 tbsp	2 tbsp
Onion, chopped	1	1	1
Small cauliflower, cut in florets	1	1	1
Carrots, sliced	2	2	2
Medium potatoes, diced	3	3	3
Mushrooms, sliced	100 g	4 oz	1 cup
Pot barley	175 g	6 oz	1 cup
Vegetable stock	600 ml	1 pint	2½ cups
Bay leaf	1	1	1
Chopped fresh parsley	2 tbsp	2 tbsp	2 tbsp
Tamari or shoyu	1 tsp	1 tsp	1 tsp
Freshly ground black pepper			

1 Heat the oil in a large saucepan and sauté the onion for about 5 minutes or until soft. Add the remaining vegetables and the barley and stir well.
2 Pour the stock, herbs and tamari or shoyu into the pan, season to taste with black pepper and leave overnight to allow the flavours to mingle and the barley to soften.
3 Next day, bring the stew to the boil and simmer gently until the stock is absorbed and the vegetables cooked.
4 Serve in warmed bowls with crusty wholewheat bread.

NOTE
If preferred, you can cook the stew in a preheated oven at 150°C/300°F (Gas Mark 2) for about 2 hours.

TONY'S JACKET POTATOES

Tony Hutchinson is a 40-year-old who runs 30 miles per week. A new convert to the sport, he finds he needs the extra carbohydrate from potatoes to supply him with that extra energy.

Serves 2	Metric	Imperial	American
Large potatoes, scrubbed	2	2	2
Skimmed milk	300 ml + 3 tbsp	½ pint + 3 tbsp	1¼ cups + 3 tbsp
Bay leaf	1	1	1
Small onion, chopped	1	1	1
Celery stalk, chopped	1	1	1
Freshly ground black pepper			
Plain wholewheat flour	1 heaped tbsp	1 heaped tbsp	1 heaped tbsp
Smoked mackerel, skinned	225 g	8 oz	½ lb
Sliced mushrooms	100 g	4 oz	1 cup

1 Bake the potatoes in a preheated oven at 200°C/400°F (Gas Mark 6) for about 1 hour or until soft.
2 Meanwhile, place the 300 ml/½ pint/1¼ cups milk, the bay leaf, onion, celery and pepper to taste in a small saucepan and bring to the boil. Simmer gently for 2 minutes.
3 Mix the flour to a paste with the remaining 3 tbsp milk and stir into the pan. Return to the boil, stirring constantly, then lower the heat and simmer for 3 minutes.
4 Cut the mackerel into chunks and add to the pan with the mushrooms. Stir to mix.
5 when cooked, cut the jacket potatoes in half and place on warmed serving plates. Top with the hot sauce and serve at once with vegetables or a mixed salad.

VARIATION
Substitute tuna for the mackerel. Vegetarians may add 50 g/2 oz/½ cup chopped walnuts.

HAPPY-GO-LUCKY PIZZA

Keith Nelson is the Editor of *Athletics Weekly* and also an accomplished athlete who doesn't eat meat. He doesn't normally measure the ingredients for his pizzas, which frequently happen to be made up of leftover vegetables. "I get bored with rigid schedules and prefer a more relaxed approach to running and eating," he says. With careful timing, these pizzas can be prepared before and between running and showering.

Serves 1	Metric	Imperial	American
Wholewheat pizza base	1	1	1
Tomato purée (paste)	4 tbsp	4 tbsp	4 tbsp
Dried herbs or chilli powder, to taste			
Canned red kidney beans, drained	2 tbsp	2 tbsp	2 tbsp
Canned sweetcorn (whole kernel corn)	2 tbsp	2 tbsp	2 tbsp
Few slices of green pepper			
Small onion, chopped	1	1	1
Mushrooms, sliced	3–4	3–4	3–4
Tomato, sliced	1	1	1
Grated cheese	50 g	2 oz	½ cup

1 Place the pizza base on a greased baking sheet. Mix the tomato purée with the herbs or chilli and spread over the pizza.
2 Scatter the beans and sweetcorn over and arrange the pepper, onion, mushrooms and tomato over them. Finally, cover with the grated cheese. Bake in a preheated oven at 220°C/425°F (Gas Mark 7) for 20–30 minutes or until bubbling.

EASY CHEESE AND TOMATO PIZZA

If it's speed you're after, this must be one of the quickest ways to produce a pizza. Margaret Aurback uses it regularly and it certainly works for her as she's one of the fastest veterans in the South East of England. Her 2 hour 48 minute marathon and 1 hour 17 minute half-marathon confirm that she must be reaping the rewards of her wholefood diet. Of course the 60–70 miles per week consistent training probably helps too!

Serves 1	Metric	Imperial	American
For the scone base			
Self-raising wholewheat flour	100 g	4 oz	1 cup
Vegetable margarine	25 g	1 oz	2 tbsp
Free-range egg, beaten	1	1	1
Skimmed milk	4 tbsp	4 tbsp	4 tbsp
For the filling			
Canned tomatoes or sliced fresh	75 g	3 oz	3 oz
Mozzarella cheese, sliced	50 g	2 oz	2 oz
Mixed dried herbs	1 tsp	1 tsp	1 tsp
Freshly ground black pepper			

1 For the scone base, sift the flour into a bowl and rub (cut) in the margarine until the mixture resembles breadcrumbs. Add the beaten egg and milk and mix well until smooth. (If preferred, the scone dough can be made by putting all the ingredients together in a food processor.)
2 Spread the dough evenly in a lightly greased 23 cm/9 inch round cake tin (pan).
3 Cover the base with the tomatoes and slices of cheese. Sprinkle over the herbs and pepper and bake in a preheated oven at 230°C/425°F (Gas Mark 7) for 20 minutes or until the dough is cooked. Serve with a large mixed salad.

POTATO AND CELERY GOULASH

Serves 4	Metric	Imperial	American
Old potatoes	1 kg	2 lb	2 lb
Sunflower oil	2 tbsp	2 tbsp	2 tbsp
Large onions, sliced	2	2	2
Celery stalks, sliced	4	4	4
Paprika	1 tbsp	1 tbsp	1 tbsp
Cumin seeds	1 tsp	1 tsp	1 tsp
Water	150 ml	¼ pint	⅔ cup
Tomato purée (paste)	1 tbsp	1 tbsp	1 tbsp
Small carton of sour cream (optional)	1	1	1

1 Wash and dry the potatoes and cut into large bite-sized pieces.
2 Heat the oil in a large saucepan or steamer and sauté the onions for about 5 minutes or until transparent. Add the potatoes and celery and continue cooking for a further 5 minutes, stirring continuously. Stir in the paprika and cumin seeds and cook for 2 minutes more.
3 Mix the water with the tomato purée and pour over the potatoes. Simmer gently for about 30 minutes or until cooked. (If preferred, cook for only 6 minutes in a pressure cooker.)
4 Stir in the sour cream, if using, and serve piping hot in warmed bowls.

NUTRITION NOTE
By leaving the skins on the potatoes you increase the amount of carbohydrate in the dish. Eat just three small potatoes and you'll receive your daily vitamin C requirement. Don't store them for too long, though — they can lose half their vitamin C content within 3 months.

POTATO BEAN BAKE

Serves 4	Metric	Imperial	American
Old potatoes	1 kg	2 lb	2 lb
400 g/14 oz can red kidney beans	1	1	1
Bunch of spring onions (scallions), sliced	1	1	1
Skimmed milk	150 ml	¼ pint	⅔ cup
Plain yoghurt	150 ml	¼ pint	⅔ cup
Dried thyme	1 tsp	1 tsp	1 tsp
Freshly ground black pepper			
Grated Cheddar cheese	175 g	6 oz	1½ cups
Wholewheat breadcrumbs	100 g	4 oz	2 cups
Rolled oats	50 g	2 oz	½ cup

1 Wash and dry the potatoes and slice thinly. Place a layer in the bottom of a greased casserole.
2 Drain the red kidney beans, rinse them to remove the brine, drain again, then spoon half over the potatoes. Sprinkle the spring onions over the beans. Continue to layer potatoes and beans, ending with a layer of potatoes.
3 Mix together the milk, yoghurt, thyme, pepper to taste, and 100 g/4 oz/1 cup of the cheese, and pour over the potatoes.
4 Mix the breadcrumbs, rolled oats and remaining cheese and sprinkle over the casserole. Bake in a preheated oven at 200°C/400°F (Gas Mark 6) for 30 minutes. Serve with green vegetables.

NUTRITION NOTE
The addition of oats to the topping provides a supply of magnesium and zinc. Red kidney beans supply iron, and the potatoes B vitamins, making this highly nutritious.

PIZZA ROLLS

Serves 4	Metric	Imperial	American
Olive oil	2 tbsp	2 tbsp	2 tbsp
Onion, chopped	1	1	1
Garlic clove, crushed	1	1	1
400 g/14 oz can tomatoes	1	1	1
Dried basil	½ tsp	½ tsp	½ tsp
Dried oregano	1 tsp	1 tsp	1 tsp
Tomato purée (paste)	3 tbsp	3 tbsp	3 tbsp
Large wholewheat baguettes	4	4	4
Canned pilchards or mackerel	100 g	4 oz	¼ lb
Stoned (pitted) green or black olives	50 g	2 oz	⅓ cup
Grated Mozzarella cheese	75 g	3 oz	¾ cup

1 Heat 1 tbsp of the olive oil in a saucepan and sauté
   the onion and garlic for about 5 minutes or until soft.
   Stir in the tomatoes with their juice, herbs and tomato
   purée, and simmer for 15 minutes or until thickened.
2 Meanwhile, cut a thin horizontal slice from the top of
   each baguette and reserve. Scoop out the bread and use
   to make breadcrumbs. Reserve. Brush the bread shells
   with the remaining olive oil and place under a hot grill
   (broiler) until just beginning to brown.
3 Roughly chop the fish and add to the tomato sauce
   with the breadcrumbs and olives. Fill each baguette
   with sauce, cover with the grated Mozzarella cheese
   and replace the 'lids'. Arrange on a greased baking
   tray and bake in a preheated oven at 180°C/350°F (Gas
   Mark 4) for 25 minutes. Serve hot with a green salad.

VARIATIONS

This is an extremely adaptable recipe — nuts, beans,
leftover meat or chicken can all replace the fish.

HUGH'S POTATO BAKE

Hugh Bergstrom must possess one of the fastest metabolic rates on the road today. Now in his 60th year, he's just relinquished his posts as Chairman of Burnham Joggers and Race Director of the Burnham Beaches Half Marathon in an attempt to break his 3 hour 11 minute marathon time.

Serves 2	Metric	Imperial	American
Large potatoes	6	6	6
Small knob of low-fat margarine	1	1	1
Freshly ground black pepper			
Can of tuna, drained and flaked	1	1	1
Tomato	1	1	1
Edam cheese, grated	100 g	4 oz	¼ lb

1 Cook the potatoes in their skins in boiling water for about 20 minutes or until tender. Allow to cool slightly before peeling. Mash the potatoes and beat in the margarine and pepper to taste.
2 Stir the tuna into the mashed potato and spoon into a casserole. Smooth the surface.
3 Slice the tomato and arrange on top of the potato.
4 Sprinkle over the grated cheese and pop under a hot grill (broiler) for a few minutes or until browned and bubbling. Alternatively, re-heat the bake in the oven at 190°C/375°F (Gas Mark 5) for about 20 minutes. Serve with a green salad or vegetables.

VARIATION
Any cooked meat or beans may be substituted for the tuna, which makes this dish an excellent way to use up any leftovers.

SPINACH AND ORANGE BUCKWHEAT PANCAKES

Pancakes can be prepared hours in advance and assembled when required. They freeze well or will keep for 2–3 days, covered, in the refrigerator. Alternatively, you could make up the batter and leave it to stand for an hour while you go for a run, and then cook and fill the pancakes on your return. They also provide a good vehicle for leftover food. Just chop up any cooked vegetables, etc., to use as a filling.

Makes 6–8

	Metric	Imperial	American
Free-range egg	1	1	1
Skimmed milk	300 ml	1/2 pint	1 1/4 cups
Orange juice	1 tbsp	1 tbsp	1 tbsp
Plain wholewheat flour	50 g	2 oz	1/2 cup
Buckwheat flour	50 g	2 oz	1/2 cup
Packet (package) of frozen spinach	1	1	1
Cottage cheese	100 g	4 oz	1/2 cup
Mushrooms, sliced	100 g	4 oz	1 cup
Pinch of grated nutmeg	1	1	1
Grated orange rind	2 tsp	2 tsp	2 tsp
Freshly ground black pepper			
Vegetable oil for frying			

1 Beat the egg, milk and orange juice together. Place the flours in a bowl and gradually beat in the liquid. Continue beating until smooth. (If you own a food processor, just tip everything in and blend until smooth.) Set aside for at least 1 hour.

2 Cook the spinach as instructed on the package and mix with the cottage cheese, mushrooms, nutmeg and orange rind. Season to taste with black pepper.

3 Heat a little oil in a small frying pan (skillet) and pour in sufficient batter just to cover the base of the pan. Heat until the batter begins to bubble, then flip it over and cook the other side. Slide the pancake out of the pan on to a plate. Continue in this way until all the batter has been used.

4 Place a portion of filling on each pancake and roll up. Lie the pancakes in the bottom of a greased ovenproof dish, brush lightly with oil, cover with foil and bake in a preheated oven at 190°C/375°F (Gas Mark 5) for 15 minutes.

NUTRITION NOTE
Spinach is a good source of vitamin C as well as riboflavin which aids in the 'burning' of sugar to produce energy. Buckwheat flour has a greater carbohydrate content than ordinary wholewheat, so you should really be flying after eating these!

NUTTY POTATOES

Serves 4 ·	Metric	Imperial	American
Large potatoes, scrubbed	4	4	4
Sunflower oil	1 tbsp	1 tbsp	1 tbsp
Mixed dried herbs	1 tsp	1 tsp	1 tsp
Unsalted peanuts	100 g	4 oz	½ cup
Low-fat cream cheese	225 g	8 oz	1 cup
Onion, chopped	1	1	1
Pinch of chilli powder (optional)	1	1	1
Celery stalk, chopped	1	1	1

1 Place the potatoes on a baking sheet, brush with oil and sprinkle with herbs. Bake in a preheated oven at 200°C/400°F (Gas Mark 6) for about 1 hour or until soft.
2 Mix together all the remaining ingredients. Cut the cooked potatoes in half and pile the filling on top. Return the potatoes to the oven for 5 minutes or until heated through.
3 Serve with a mixed salad.

NUTRITION NOTE
Don't leave the potato skins on your plate! The goodness in potatoes lies just beneath the surface and the skins also provide necessary fibre. Peanuts also contain fibre as well as protein, vitamins and minerals.

MEXICAN PETE'S PIZZAS

Pete Stebbing is a 20 miles-a-week runner from Manchester with an ambition to run a marathon. The carbohydrate from the beans and the pizza base will help provide him with the extra energy for increased training.

Makes 2	Metric	Imperial	American
For the pizza base			
Self-raising wholewheat flour	225 g	8 oz	2 cups
Vegetable margarine	50 g	2 oz	¼ cup
Skimmed milk	150 ml	¼ pint	⅔ cup
For the topping			
Sunflower oil	1 tbsp	1 tbsp	1 tbsp
Onion, chopped	1	1	1
Small green pepper, deseeded and chopped	1	1	1
Garlic clove, crushed	1	1	1
Dried oregano	½ tsp	½ tsp	½ tsp
Dried basil	½ tsp	½ tsp	½ tsp
Pinch of chilli powder	1	1	1
400 g/14 oz can tomatoes	1	1	1
Cooked or canned red kidney beans	100 g	4 oz	⅓ cup
Tomato purée (paste)	2 tbsp	2 tbsp	2 tbsp
Mozzarella cheese	75 g	3 oz	3 oz

1 To make the base, place the flour in a large bowl and rub (cut) in the margarine until the mixture resembles breadcrumbs. Stir in the milk and mix to a dough.
2 Turn the dough on to a floured surface and cut in half. Roll out to form two rounds about 15 cm/6 inches across.
3 Heat the oil in a small frying pan (skillet) and sauté the onion, pepper and garlic for 5–10 minutes or until just soft. Stir in the herbs and spices and cook for a further 2 minutes.
4 Mix together the tomatoes with their juice, the beans and purée. Pour on to the onions, peppers and spices and mix well.

5 Place the pizza bases on a greased baking sheet and spread the topping evenly over each. Slice the Mozzarella and arrange on top. Bake in a preheated oven at 200°C/400°F (Gas Mark 6) for about 30 minutes or until the cheese is bubbling. Serve with a salad.

NUTRITION NOTE
Mozzarella cheese is fairly high in fat so, if you aim to eat these pizzas frequently, experiment with a low-fat alternative such as Edam.

WHEAT BERRY PILAFF

Serves 4	Metric	Imperial	American
Vegetable stock	900 ml	1½ pints	3¾ cups
Wheat berries, soaked overnight	225 g	8 oz	½ lb
Sunflower oil	2 tbsp	2 tbsp	2 tbsp
Onion, chopped	1	1	1
Garlic clove, crushed	1	1	1
Chopped celery	4 tbsp	4 tbsp	4 tbsp
Mushrooms, sliced	100 g	4 oz	1 cup
Red pepper, deseeded and chopped	½	½	½
Green pepper, deseeded and chopped	½	½	½
Soya sauce	1 tsp	1 tsp	1 tsp
Chopped fresh parsley	2 tbsp	2 tbsp	2 tbsp

1 Put the vegetable stock in a large saucepan and bring to the boil. Add the wheat berries and simmer for about 1 hour or until tender.
2 Meanwhile, heat the oil in a frying pan (skillet) and sauté the onion and garlic for about 5 minutes or until transparent.
3 Add the remaining vegetables and cook gently for a further 2–3 minutes.
4 Drain the wheat berries and stir into the vegetables. Add the soya sauce and parsley and mix well.
5 Serve as an alternative to rice.

PULSE POWER

Think of a food that is high in fibre and carbohydrate, contains twice the protein of meat, four times the protein of eggs and 12 times the protein of milk, and is also a rich source of B vitamins. Yes, the modest, under-rated soya bean can claim to provide all these nutrients, but the whole pulse family is a rich store-cupboard. Pulses are the seeds of legumes and include beans, peas and lentils. Once they were regarded as second class proteins but they have now been promoted to first class. And first class they certainly are when you consider the variety of dishes you can make with them and the low cost of buying them.

Nutritionally, pulses are a valuable addition to the runner's diet because they contain significant amounts of vitamin B_6 (pyridoxine) which aids in the conversion of glycogen to energy. Thiamin (B_1) is also present, and if you're running low on this vitamin you will experience that heavy-legged feeling caused by a build-up of lactic acid in the muscles. Those on a high-carbo diet (and that should include all of us), and those who drink alcohol regularly, require more thiamin than the average person. It therefore follows that those who run and drink should eat a few beans, preferably in that order!

Pulses cannot provide 'complete' proteins when eaten on their own because they don't contain the full range of amino acids. However, this is a simple problem to remedy. All you have to do is serve them with some form of grains, dairy produce, wholewheat flour, nuts or seeds to make up the whole protein. You'll find you will do uhis quite naturally anyway, beans on toast being the classic example.

A word of caution if you are just introducing pulses into your diet for the first time: Some runners do suffer from flatulence as a result of eating pulses until their systems adjust to the extra fibre. My advice is to eat them sparingly to begin with, unless you intend to run your races jet-propelled or wind-assisted!

MACARONI AND BEAN SOUP

Serves 4	Metric	Imperial	American
Olive oil	*2 tbsp*	*2 tbsp*	*2 tbsp*
Cooked haricot (navy) beans	*175 g*	*6 oz*	*1 cup*
Carrots, sliced	*2*	*2*	*2*
Large onion, chopped	*1*	*1*	*1*
Celery stalks, sliced	*2*	*2*	*2*
Medium leek, sliced	*1*	*1*	*1*
Garlic cloves, crushed	*2*	*2*	*2*
Vegetable stock	*1.75 litres*	*3 pints*	*7½ cups*
Tomato purée (paste)	*1 tbsp*	*1 tbsp*	*1 tbsp*
Tamari	*1 tsp*	*1 tsp*	*1 tsp*
Dried basil	*1 tsp*	*1 tsp*	*1 tsp*
Wholewheat short-cut (elbow) macaroni	*100 g*	*4 oz*	*1 cup*
Freshly ground black pepper			
Chopped fresh parsley	*2 tbsp*	*2 tbsp*	*2 tbsp*
Grated Parmesan cheese			

1 Heat the oil in a large saucepan and sauté the vegetables for 2–3 minutes.
2 Mix the stock with the tomato purée, tamari and basil and pour over the vegetables. Bring to the boil, then lower the heat and simmer gently for about 45 minutes or until the vegetables are cooked.
3 Add the macaroni and simmer for a further 8–10 minutes or until tender. Season to taste with pepper and serve in warmed bowls with fresh parsley and Parmesan sprinkled over. Serve with plenty of crusty wholewheat bread.

NUTRITION NOTE
This is a really high-fibre soup and an ideal carbohydrate supply after a hard training session. It's perfect for those who can't face a heavy meal immediately after running.

VEGETABLE COUSCOUS

This sustaining vegetable stew has, for many years, satisfied hungry joggers at our club, where it is cooked by Joan Corbishly. She's a 53-year-old grandmother who trains 35 miles per week and has a half marathon personal best of 1 hour 59 minutes.

Serves 6	Metric	Imperial	American
Couscous	450 g	1 lb	1 lb
Water	1 litre	2 pints	5 cups
Vegetable oil	50 ml	2 fl oz	¼ cup
Medium onions, quartered	2	2	2
Medium green peppers, deseeded and cut into thick strips	2	2	2
Small courgettes (zucchini), cut into 2.5 cm/1 inch pieces	6	6	6
Large potatoes, scrubbed and coarsely chopped	2	2	2
Small turnips, halved and thickly sliced	2	2	2
Medium carrots, cut in half horizontally, then sliced vertically	4	4	4
Garlic cloves, crushed	3	3	3
Small chillies, deseeded and chopped	2	2	2
Chick-peas, cooked	225 g	8 oz	1⅓ cups
Canned tomatoes	450 g	1 lb	1 lb
Ground coriander	1½ tsp	1½ tsp	1½ tsp
Ground cumin	1½ tsp	1½ tsp	1½ tsp
Ground turmeric	2 tsp	2 tsp	2 tsp
Cayenne pepper	½ tsp	½ tsp	½ tsp
Sultanas (golden raisins), raisins or no-need-to-soak dried apricots	100 g	4 oz	¼ lb

1 Place the couscous in a large bowl and stir in half the
   water. Drain immediately, then leave the couscous for
   about 10 minutes to allow the grains to swell. Fork out
   any lumps.
2 Meanwhile, heat the oil in the base of a steamer or
   couscousier. Add all the vegetables but not the tomatoes,
   and sauté for 10 minutes. Add the remaining water,
   bring to the boil and simmer for 30 minutes.
3 Turn the couscous into the top of the steamer or
   couscousier and place over the vegetables to steam for
   30 minutes.
4 Remove the top of the steamer or couscousier and add
   the spices, tomatoes and dried fruit to the vegetables.
   Bring to the boil, then reduce the heat and simmer for
   20 minutes. Replace the top of the steamer or
   couscousier and steam the couscous for a final
   20 minutes.
5 Serve the grains in warmed individual bowls with the
   vegetables over the top.

VARIATIONS
The vegetable mixture is just as delicious served with rice
or potatoes, and you can use any vegetables in season.

ROOT AND LENTIL CASSEROLE

Jill Danskin is yet more proof that you don't need red meat to produce classy performances. She has a 2 hour 56 minute marathon under her belt and a string of international competitions. A native of Dundee, it must be the canny Scot in her that sees the sense of a vegetarian diet.

Serves 4	Metric	Imperial	American
Sunflower oil	*3 tbsp*	*3 tbsp*	*3 tbsp*
Root vegetables, diced	*700 g*	*1½ lb*	*1½ lb*
Celery stalks, sliced	*2*	*2*	*2*
Onions, sliced	*2*	*2*	*2*
Red lentils	*225 g*	*8 oz*	*1 cup*
Garlic cloves, crushed	*2*	*2*	*2*
Curry powder	*2 tsp*	*2 tsp*	*2 tsp*
Large tomatoes	*4*	*4*	*4*
Vegetable stock or water	*900 ml*	*1½ pints*	*3¾ cups*
Juice of ½ lemon			
Freshly ground black pepper			
Chopped fresh coriander, to garnish			

1 Heat the oil in a large, heavy-bottomed saucepan and sauté the root vegetables, celery and onions for 5 minutes.
2 Add the lentils and garlic and stir-fry for another 5 minutes. Stir in 2 tsp curry powder, or to taste, during the last 2 minutes.
3 Cut the tomatoes into wedges and add to the pan with the stock and lemon juice. Season to taste with pepper. Bring to the boil, then transfer to an ovenproof dish. Bake in a preheated oven at 200°C/400°F (Gas Mark 6) for 1 hour. Sprinkle with coriander and serve with brown rice or baked potatoes.

SAVOURY CHICK-PEAS

This recipe is a favourite of physiotherapist Fiona Russell whose claim to fame is that she once finished a race only 38 seconds behind Zola Budd. Fiona trains with Zola from time to time so it's difficult to assess whether her good form is due to her near vegan diet or her élite training partner!

Serves 2	Metric	Imperial	American
Sunflower oil	2 tbsp	2 tbsp	2 tbsp
Onion, chopped	1	1	1
Mushrooms, sliced	225 g	8 oz	2 cups
Red pepper, deseeded and chopped	1	1	1
Can of chick-peas, drained	1	1	1
Vegetable stock	4 tbsp	4 tbsp	4 tbsp
Grated nutmeg	½ tsp	½ tsp	½ tsp
Mustard	1 tsp	1 tsp	1 tsp
Cider	2 tsp	2 tsp	2 tsp
Soya sauce	1 tsp	1 tsp	1 tsp
Wholewheat noodles	175 g	6 oz	6 oz
Soya or plain yoghurt	450 ml	¾ pint	2 cups

1 Heat the oil in a large frying pan (skillet) or wok and sauté the onion for about 5 minutes or until transparent. Add the mushrooms and pepper and cook for a further 2 minutes. Stir in the chick-peas, stock, nutmeg, mustard, cider and soya sauce and simmer gently for 10–15 minutes.
2 Meanwhile, cook the noodles in boiling water for 8–10 minutes or until tender, then drain.
3 Pour the yoghurt on to the chick-peas and stir. Serve over the hot noodles with a large mixed salad.

MEXICAN BEAN STEW

Vivienne Fullerton trains in Newtownabbey, Co. Antrim, and cooks up a large pot of this before her long Sunday run. As with most stews, it tastes even better the next day, so even if you're only cooking for one person, it's worth preparing the full quantity.

Serves 4–6	Metric	Imperial	American
Vegetable oil	2 tbsp	2 tbsp	2 tbsp
Large onion, finely chopped	1	1	1
Garlic cloves, crushed	1–4	1–4	1–4
Large red pepper, deseeded and sliced	1	1	1
Large green pepper, deseeded and sliced	1	1	1
Chilli powder	2–3 tsp	2–3 tsp	2–3 tsp
Dash of Tabasco (hot pepper) sauce	1	1	1
400 g/14 oz cans chopped tomatoes	2	2	2
400 g/14 oz can red kidney beans, drained and rinsed	1	1	1
400 g/14 oz can borlotti or haricot (navy) beans, drained and rinsed	1	1	1

1 Heat the oil in a large frying pan (skillet) or wok and sauté the onion and garlic for about 5 minutes or until soft. Add the peppers and continue to cook for a further 2–3 minutes.
2 Stir in the chilli powder, Tabasco and tomatoes. Add the beans, stirring well, and bring to the boil. Lower the heat and leave the stew to simmer gently for about 30 minutes.
3 Serve with brown rice, baked potatoes or pasta.

PINTO TACOS

Serves 4	Metric	Imperial	American
Taco shells	8	8	8
Vegetable margarine	100 g	4 oz	½ cup
Large onion, chopped	1	1	1
Garlic cloves, crushed	2	2	2
Chopped fresh green chilli	1 tsp	1 tsp	1 tsp
Chopped fresh coriander	2 tbsp	2 tbsp	2 tbsp
Cooked pinto beans	350 g	12 oz	1 cup
Selection of salad vegetables			

1 Place the taco shells on a baking tray in a warm oven
   170°C/325°F (Gas Mark 3) to heat through whilst
   preparing the filling.
2 Melt 50 g/2 oz/¼ cup of the margarine in a frying pan
   (skillet) and sauté the onion, garlic and chilli for about
   5 minutes or until soft. Add the coriander and cook for a
   further 2 minutes.
3 Meanwhile, mash the beans or purée them in a food
   processor or blender. Add the onion, etc., and mash or
   re-process. The mixture should resemble mashed potato.
4 Melt the remaining margarine in the frying pan and
   quickly fry the bean mixture until it is evenly heated.
   Place a portion of beans in each taco shell and pile
   shredded lettuce, chopped cucumber, etc., on top. Serve
   with a large jug of water!

NUTRITION NOTE
The spicy nature of these tacos just might have you
running off course so enjoy them *after* a race rather than
before! The beans accompanied by the flour in the tacos
means vegetarians can be sure they're eating a complete
protein.

LENTIL AND CHEESE LAYER

Brian Moule runs with his wife around the Harley Street area of London. Living in such health-conscious environs has obviously rubbed off and this lentil dish may have contributed to his personal best 2 hour 53 minute marathon. Although, with a 10K time of 33 minutes 59 seconds, there are greater times ahead.

Serves 4	Metric	Imperial	American
Olive oil	2 tbsp	2 tbsp	2 tbsp
Chopped onion	100 g	4 oz	1 cup
Garlic cloves, crushed	2–3	2–3	2–3
Celery stalks, chopped	3	3	3
Chopped carrot	225 g	8 oz	2 cups
Red lentils	175 g	6 oz	¾ cup
Red pepper, deseeded and chopped	1	1	1
400 g/14 oz can tomatoes	1	1	1
Dried marjoram	½ tsp	½ tsp	½ tsp
Red wine (optional)	60 ml	2½ fl oz	5 tbsp
Water	175 ml	6 fl oz	¾ cup
Bay leaves	2	2	2
Freshly ground black pepper			
Vegetable margarine	25 g	1 oz	2 tbsp
Plain wholewheat flour	25 g	1 oz	¼ cup
Skimmed milk	300 ml	½ pint	1¼ cups
Grated cheese	40 g	1½ oz	⅓ cup
Large aubergine (eggplant), sliced	1	1	1
Chopped fresh parsley, to garnish			

1 Heat half the oil in a large saucepan and stir-fry the onion, garlic and celery over a low heat for 5 minutes or until soft but not brown. Stir in the carrots and cook for a further 2 minutes.
2 Stir in the lentils, red pepper, tomatoes, marjoram, red wine (if using), water (adding an extra 60 ml/2½ fl oz/5 tbsp if not using wine) and bay leaves. Cover and bring

to the boil, then reduce the heat and simmer for
35 minutes. Season to taste with black pepper.
3 Meanwhile, make a cheese sauce by melting the
margarine in a saucepan and stirring in the flour.
Remove from the heat and gradually stir in the skimmed
milk. Bring to the boil and simmer for 2–3 minutes or
until thickened, stirring continuously. Add the cheese
and stir until melted.
4 Place the aubergine slices on a baking tray and brush
with the remaining oil. Bake in a preheated oven at
180°C/350°F (Gas Mark 4) for 15–20 minutes.
Alternatively, microwave owners can cook the aubergine
slices under absorbent kitchen paper, without oil, for
3–4 minutes.
5 Place the lentil sauce in an ovenproof dish and cover
with slices of aubergine. Pour over the cheese sauce,
cover with foil and bake in a preheated oven at
190°C/375°F (Gas Mark 5) for 35–40 minutes. Garnish
with chopped parsley before serving.

HIGH CARBO BEAN PÂTÉ

Serves 6	Metric	Imperial	American
425 g/15 oz can chick-peas,			
drained	1	1	1
Tahini	4 tbsp	4 tbsp	4 tbsp
Lemon juice	2 tbsp	2 tbsp	2 tbsp
Garlic cloves, crushed	4	4	4
Olive oil	4 tbsp	4 tbsp	4 tbsp
Freshly ground black pepper			
Chopped fresh parsley	1 tbsp	1 tbsp	1 tbsp

1 Place all the ingredients in a blender or a food processor
and purée until smooth. The consistency should
resemble thick porridge. If it's too stiff, thin with a
little vegetable stock.
2 Spoon the pâte into a serving dish and chill for
several hours or overnight before serving.
3 Serve as a starter or light lunch with a selection of raw
vegetables and wholewheat toast.

BOSTON BEAN CASSEROLE

This is the ideal meal for runners as it improves with keeping. I've enjoyed many long Sunday runs knowing that a hearty meal awaits me, and the family won't go hungry if I run an extra couple of miles.

Serves 4	Metric	Imperial	American
Pinto beans	*225 g*	*8 oz*	*¾ cup*
Sunflower oil	*2 tbsp*	*2 tbsp*	*2 tbsp*
Onions, sliced	*2*	*2*	*2*
Garlic clove, crushed	*1*	*1*	*1*
Small cauliflower, broken into			
florets	*1*	*1*	*1*
Carrots, scrubbed and sliced	*2*	*2*	*2*
Small aubergine (eggplant),			
chopped	*1*	*1*	*1*
Ground cinnamon	*2 tsp*	*2 tsp*	*2 tsp*
Dried thyme	*2 tsp*	*2 tsp*	*2 tsp*
Vegetable stock	*1 litre*	*2 pints*	*5 cups*
Tomato purée (paste)	*100 g*	*4 oz*	*6 tbsp*
Freshly ground black pepper			

1 Soak the beans in cold water overnight.
2 Drain the beans, put in a saucepan and cover with fresh cold water. Bring to the boil and cook for about 1 hour or until tender, then set aside.
3 Heat the oil in a frying pan (skillet) and sauté the onions and garlic for about 5 minutes or until soft. Add all the other vegetables and stir-fry for 5 minutes. Stir in the cinnamon and thyme and continue cooking for a further 2–3 minutes.
4 Blend the stock with the tomato purée and pour on to the vegetables. Add the cooked beans and simmer gently for at least 20 minutes or until the vegetables are tender.
5 Season to taste with pepper and serve with brown rice.

ALL IN A NUTSHELL

To most of us, nuts come in small packets, ready salted, dry roasted or spiced. They're served with pre-dinner drinks or lurk in small bowls on the bar counter. They are hardly the sort of ingredient a hungry runner would consider or relish eating as part of a high-energy diet. Yet they're packed with protein, fibre, vitamins and minerals.

The reason why many people avoid nuts is their high calorie count. At 150–200 cals per 25 g/1 oz it's very easy to pile on the pounds. If you're not calorie counting, the protein content of nuts is greater than fish, meat, chicken, beans or milk and they're a convenient snack food. The safest way to eat them is in cooked dishes because the amount required to satisfy is extremely small.

The other reason we avoid nuts is that they contain a lot of fat, but it is unsaturated fat. Coconut is the only exception, with its 80 per cent saturated fat, and definitely deserves the red light. Watch out for it in 'trail mix' and those non-dairy creamers which use coconut as a base.

Women in particular, it seems, may benefit from including nuts in their diet if the results of an American study are to be believed. Apparently nuts can bring about changes in oestrogen levels which could relieve painful or troublesome periods. Almonds, cashews and peanuts have been found to be the most effective.

One area of caution must be the pre-race situation, especially for runners with nervous bowels. The high fat content of nuts means that they move slowly through the digestive system and just may catch you unawares!

AUBERGINE WITH ALMONDS

Serves 4	Metric	Imperial	American
Medium aubergines (eggplants)	2	2	2
Olive oil	1 tbsp	1 tbsp	1 tbsp
Onion, chopped	1	1	1
Garlic clove, crushed	1	1	1
Red pepper, deseeded and diced	½	½	½
Mushrooms, sliced	50 g	2 oz	½ cup
Ground coriander	1 tsp	1 tsp	1 tsp
Ground cumin	1 tsp	1 tsp	1 tsp
Ground turmeric	½ tsp	½ tsp	½ tsp
Garam masala	1 tsp	1 tsp	1 tsp
Chilli powder (optional)	½ tsp	½ tsp	½ tsp
Tomato purée (paste)	1 tbsp	1 tbsp	1 tbsp
Cooked brown rice	100 g	4 oz	¾ cup
Sultanas (golden raisins)	25 g	1 oz	3 tbsp
Flaked (slivered) almonds	50 g	2 oz	½ cup
Grated Parmesan cheese			
Red pepper slices			

1 Preheat the oven at its highest setting. Cut each aubergine in half lengthways and make a slit down the centre of the flesh of each. Place them on a greased baking sheet and cook in the oven for 15 minutes. Remove from the oven and leave to cool.
2 When the aubergines are cool, scoop out the flesh and chop. Reserve the skins.
3 Heat the oil in a frying pan (skillet) and stir-fry the onion and garlic for about 5 minutes or until soft. Add the red pepper, mushrooms and aubergine and continue to cook until just beginning to soften.
4 Stir in the spices, tomato purée, rice, sultanas and nuts and cook for a further 2–3 minutes. Add a little water if the mixture is too dry.
5 Divide the mixture between the aubergine skins, sprinkle with the Parmesan and top with slices of red pepper. Bake in the oven at 180°C/350°F (Gas Mark 4) for 20 minutes or until well browned.

LEEKS IN WALNUT SAUCE

Most of this tasty supper dish can be prepared before you run and then assembled when you return.

Serves 2	Metric	Imperial	American
Walnut pieces	50 g	2 oz	½ cup
400 g/14 oz can tomatoes	1	1	1
Tomato purée (paste)	2 tbsp	2 tbsp	2 tbsp
Small onion	1	1	1
Dash of Tabasco (hot pepper) sauce	1	1	1
Dried oregano	2 tsp	2 tsp	2 tsp
Dried basil	2 tsp	2 tsp	2 tsp
Water	150 ml	¼ pint	⅔ cup
Sunflower oil	2 tbsp	2 tbsp	2 tbsp
Large leeks, sliced	2	2	2
Garlic cloves, crushed	2	2	2
Medium carrots, cut into sticks	2	2	2

1 Place the walnuts, tomatoes, tomato purée and onion in a blender or food processor and purée for 1 minute. Transfer to a bowl and stir in the Tabasco, herbs and water.
2 Heat the oil in a large frying pan (skillet) or wok and stir-fry the leeks, garlic and carrots for 8–10 minutes or until tender.
3 Pour the walnut sauce over the vegetables and heat through. Serve with pasta, baked potatoes and wholewheat grains.

VARIATION
The basic sauce can be used with almost any combination of vegetables, although leeks are a good source of folic acid and potassium.

CAULIFLOWER NUT BAKE

Ann Barclay from Durham, in the North East of England, invented this tasty method of serving cauliflower. You can add any cooked vegetable to the nut base.

Serves 4	Metric	Imperial	American
Large cauliflower	*1*	*1*	*1*
Vegetable oil			
Onion, chopped	*1*	*1*	*1*
Garlic clove, crushed	*1*	*1*	*1*
Ground coriander	*2 tsp*	*2 tsp*	*2 tsp*
Ground turmeric	*1 tsp*	*1 tsp*	*1 tsp*
Peeled and grated fresh root ginger	*1 tsp*	*1 tsp*	*1 tsp*
Wholewheat breadcrumbs	*175 g*	*6 oz*	*3 cups*
Grated cheese	*50 g*	*2 oz*	*½ cup*
Ground hazelnuts	*100 g*	*4 oz*	*1 cup*
Vegetable margarine	*50 g*	*2 oz*	*¼ cup*
Plain wholewheat flour	*50 g*	*2 oz*	*½ cup*
Mustard powder	*1 tsp*	*1 tsp*	*1 tsp*
Skimmed milk	*300 ml*	*½ pint*	*1¼ cups*
Tomatoes	*2*	*2*	*2*

1 Break the cauliflower into florets and cook in boiling water for about 8 minutes or until just tender, taking care not to overcook it. Drain and set aside.
2 Heat a little oil in a small frying pan (skillet) and gently sauté the onion and garlic for 5 minutes or until soft. Add the spices and stir-fry for 2–3 minutes.
3 Mix the breadcrumbs, cheese and hazelnuts and add the onion and spices. Mix well and press into the bottom of an ovenproof dish.
4 Make the mustard sauce by melting the margarine in a small saucepan. Stir in the flour and mustard powder and cook for 2 minutes, stirring. Remove from the heat and gradually stir in the milk. Bring to the boil and cook for 2–3 minutes or until smooth and thick, stirring continuously. Remove from the heat.
5 Arrange the cooked cauliflower on the nut base and

pour the mustard sauce over the top. Slice the tomatoes
and arrange round the edge. Bake in a preheated oven at
220°C/425°F (Gas Mark 7) for 15 minutes or until brown.

WALNUT AND VEGETABLE PILAU

Serves 4	Metric	Imperial	American
Sunflower oil	2 tbsp	2 tbsp	2 tbsp
Onions, sliced	2	2	2
Garlic clove, crushed	1	1	1
Large carrots, thinly sliced	3	3	3
Small parsnips, thinly sliced	2	2	2
Walnut pieces	100 g	4 oz	1 cup
Shelled peas	100 g	4 oz	¾ cup
400 g/14 oz can tomatoes	1	1	1
Mushrooms, sliced	100 g	4 oz	1 cup
Ground cumin	1 tsp	1 tsp	1 tsp
Ground coriander	1 tsp	1 tsp	1 tsp
Ground turmeric	½ tsp	½ tsp	½ tsp
Garam masala	½ tsp	½ tsp	½ tsp
Chilli powder (optional)	½ tsp	½ tsp	½ tsp
Ground cinnamon	1 tsp	1 tsp	1 tsp
Tomato purée (paste)	1 tbsp	1 tbsp	1 tbsp
Brown rice, cooked	225 g	8 oz	1¼ cups

1 Heat the oil in a large frying pan (skillet) or wok and
   sauté the onion and garlic for about 5 minutes or until
   transparent. Add all the vegetables, except the peas,
   tomatoes and mushrooms, and stir-fry for 10–15 minutes
   or until just beginning to soften.
2 Stir in the walnuts, peas and mushrooms and continue
   cooking for a further 2–3 minutes.
3 In a small bowl, combine the spices and canned tomato
   juice. When well mixed, add to the pan with the
   tomatoes and tomato purée.
4 When the vegetables are cooked, remove from the heat
   and serve over the brown rice.

CASHEW AND APRICOT ROAST

Serves 6–8	Metric	Imperial	American
Cashew nut pieces	225 g	8 oz	2 cups
Wholewheat breadcrumbs	100 g	4 oz	2 cups
Sunflower oil	2 tbsp	2 tbsp	2 tbsp
Onions, chopped	2	2	2
Celery stalks, chopped	2	2	2
Small red pepper, deseeded and chopped	1	1	1
Garlic cloves, crushed	4	4	4
Dried thyme	4 tsp	4 tsp	4 tsp
Dried basil	3 tsp	3 tsp	3 tsp
Dried oregano	2 tsp	2 tsp	2 tsp
Free-range eggs, beaten	2	2	2
Skimmed milk	150 ml	¼ pint	⅔ cup
Freshly ground black pepper			
No-need-to-soak dried apricots, chopped	100 g	4 oz	⅔ cup

For the garnish
Watercress sprigs
Red pepper slices

1 Grind the nuts in a blender or food processor and mix with the breadcrumbs.
2 Heat the oil in a frying pan (skillet) and sauté the onion, celery, red pepper and garlic for 5–10 minutes or until soft. Stir in the herbs and add to the nuts and breadcrumbs.
3 Whisk the eggs and milk together and pour into the mixture. Stir well and season to taste with black pepper.
4 Place half the nut mixture in the base of a greased and lined 1 kg/2 lb loaf tin (pan). Follow with a layer of all the chopped apricots and cover with the remaining nut mixture.
5 Bake in a preheated oven at 200°C/400°F (Gas Mark 6) for 35–40 minutes. Turn out onto a large serving dish and garnish with watercress and slices of red pepper. Serve with a favourite sauce.

NOTE

Nuts eaten in this way do not pile on the calories. This Cashew and apricot roast is extremely filling and even the hungriest runner should be satisfied with one helping!

HERBED ROASTED NUTS

Serves 4	Metric	Imperial	American
Mixed whole nuts	*100 g*	*4 oz*	*1 cup*
Vegetable margarine	*25 g*	*1 oz*	*2 tbsp*
Dried rosemary	*½ tbsp*	*½ tbsp*	*½ tbsp*
Dried thyme	*½ tsp*	*½ tsp*	*½ tsp*
Dried marjoram	*½ tsp*	*½ tsp*	*½ tsp*
Ground allspice	*½ tsp*	*½ tsp*	*½ tsp*
Pinch of cayenne pepper	*1*	*1*	*1*

1 Mix together all the ingredients and place on a greased baking sheet.
2 Bake in a preheated oven at 180°C/350°F (Gas Mark 4) for 10–15 minutes, stirring once.
3 Serve across the bar or with pre-dinner drinks.

VERSATILE VEGGIES AND SAVOURIES

Vegetable dishes are a boon to the runner with one eye on the clock and the other on his/her cholesterol level. More and more runners are turning their backs on animal flesh and taking the first tentative steps towards a healthier diet. Even if total vegetarianism is not for you, most experts agree that cutting down on animal fats and eating more fresh vegetables makes nutritional sense.

Eating a wide variety of vegetables is the way to ensure a steady supply of the essential vitamins and minerals your body needs. It's a much cheaper and simpler method of guaranteeing supplies than popping lots of pills. Don't be satisfied with the old favourites, such as peas and cabbage; live dangerously and discover the diverse flavours of aubergines (eggplants), spinach or okra.

The popularity of the wok has cut cooking time to a minimum and it's now possible to produce an almost instant meal of stir-fry vegetables. Throw in a few of your favourite herbs or spices and serve with a whole grain. The whole operation is quicker and safer than a trip to the burger bar.

Microwave cooking is not only time saving, but also produces vegetables that are crispier and crunchier than those which have been boiled or steamed. Vegetables cooked in a microwave oven retain more nutrients than when cooked by any other method.

Whenever possible, scrub rather than peel vegetables and only buy the freshest. There's very little goodness in a limp and yellowed cabbage. Many vitamins and minerals are water soluble so use cooking water for soups, sauces and gravy.

When it comes to savouries, cheese and eggs spring first to mind but learn to treat them with caution. Be economical with hard cheeses and restrict eggs to three per week. Both foods in excess will almost certainly increase your cholesterol levels, clog your arteries and ultimately slow you down in life's long run.

HERBED CHEESE SAVOURY

Alton Jogger, Mary Rumsey, who is over 50 years old, runs 20 miles per week and has competed over most distances up to the marathon. She devised this very simple cheese savoury when a friend on a diet came to lunch. Any vegetables can be used, e.g. leeks, mushrooms or green peppers, but avoid tomatoes which add too much moisture.

Serves 2	Metric	Imperial	American
Vegetable oil or stock			
Large onion, chopped	*1*	*1*	*1*
Free-range eggs, separated	*2*	*2*	*2*
Low-fat curd cheese	*100 g*	*4 oz*	*½ cup*
Cottage cheese	*100 g*	*4 oz*	*½ cup*
Low-fat plain yoghurt	*150 ml*	*¼ pint*	*⅔ cup*
Cornflour (cornstarch)	*25 g*	*1 oz*	*¼ cup*
Mixed dried herbs	*2 tsp*	*2 tsp*	*2 tsp*

1 Heat a little oil in a frying pan (skillet) and sauté the onion for about 5 minutes or until soft. Alternatively, to avoid using extra fat, cook the onion in a little boiling vegetable stock until just tender. Drain well.
2 Beat the egg whites until stiff. Beat together the egg yolks, curd cheese, cottage cheese, yoghurt, cornflour and herbs until well mixed and fairly smooth. Stir in the onion, then fold in the egg whites.
3 Spoon the mixture into a well oiled ovenproof dish and bake in a preheated oven at 200°C/400°F (Gas Mark 6) for 20–30 minutes or until risen and browned. Serve with a large salad and baked potatoes.

COURGETTE AND TOMATO QUICHE

Quiches can be cooked well ahead and are ideal with salads after summer training runs. Denise Howse, who runs for Burnham Joggers, one of the largest of the new breed of running clubs in England, can always be relied upon to produce a delicious quiche for one of their many social events. In between socializing she's managed a 1 hour 26 minute half marathon and a 39 minute 10K.

Serves 4	Metric	Imperial	American
23 cm/9 inch uncooked wholewheat pastry flan case (pie shell)	1	1	1
Vegetable margarine	50 g	2 oz	¼ cup
Garlic cloves, crushed	2	2	2
Medium courgettes (zucchini), sliced	4	4	4
Dried oregano	½ tsp	½ tsp	½ tsp
Freshly ground black pepper			
Skimmed milk	120 ml	4 fl oz	½ cup
Skimmed milk powder	15 g	½ oz	½ oz
Free-range eggs	3	3	3
Grated Edam cheese	50 g	2 oz	½ cup
Small tomatoes, sliced	5	5	5

1 Place the flan case on a baking sheet and set aside.
2 Melt the margarine in a frying pan (skillet) and gently sauté the garlic for 1 minute. Add the courgettes and stir-fry for 5 minutes or until they are lightly browned. Remove from the heat and stir in the oregano and black pepper to taste.
3 Combine the milk, milk powder, eggs and cheese, beating well to blend.
4 Arrange the courgettes and tomatoes in the base of the flan case and pour over the egg and milk mixture. Bake in a preheated oven at 200°C/400°F (Gas Mark 6) for 35–40 minutes or until the filling is set and golden. Serve hot or cold.

VARIATIONS

To boost carbohydrate, fibre and protein, try adding 25 g/ 1 oz/¼ cup soya flour or rolled oats to your pastry. Vary the quiche filling by adding 100 g/4 oz/¼ lb cooked or canned red kidney beans and a pinch of cayenne.

COURGETTE CURRY

Ian Thompson and his wife Margaret have developed this curry. Although Ian says he has a tendency to throw in whatever is to hand, Margaret is more consistent and measures the spices accurately. Whichever attitude you adopt, I can't guarantee that you'll have the same running success as them. Ian averages 80 miles per week, hoping to recapture the performance which made him Commonwealth and European marathon champion with a personal best of 2 hours 9 minutes. Margaret averages 30 miles per week and has produced a 57 minute 10-mile time.

Serves 3–4	Metric	Imperial	American
Vegetable oil	2 tbsp	2 tbsp	2 tbsp
Garlic clove, crushed	1	1	1
Ground coriander	2 tsp	2 tsp	2 tsp
Ground cumin	1 tsp	1 tsp	1 tsp
Chilli powder	½ tsp	½ tsp	½ tsp
Water	2 tbsp	2 tbsp	2 tbsp
Courgettes (zucchini), sliced	450 g	1 lb	1 lb
Potatoes, cut into small pieces	225 g	8 oz	½ lb

1 Heat the oil in a saucepan and quickly sauté the garlic and spices for about 2 minutes, stirring constantly. Stir in the water and cook gently for a further 2 minutes.
2 Add the vegetables, cover and simmer gently for 45 minutes–1 hour or until soft. Serve with plenty of nan bread or brown rice.

NOTE

You can add salt to this if you must.

TAIL END VEGGIES

Serves 2	Metric	Imperial	American
Sunflower oil	2 tbsp	2 tbsp	2 tbsp
Small cabbage, cut in strips	¼	¼	¼
Medium carrot, cut in thin sticks	1	1	1
Onion, sliced	1	1	1
Garlic clove, crushed	1	1	1
Celery stalk, sliced	1	1	1
Green pepper, deseeded and sliced	½	½	½
Red pepper, deseeded and sliced	½	½	½
Large mushrooms, sliced	3–4	3–4	3–4
Tomato purée (paste)	1 tbsp	1 tbsp	1 tbsp
Wine vinegar	1 tbsp	1 tbsp	1 tbsp
Miso (barley)	3 tsp	3 tsp	3 tsp
Vegetable stock or water	300 ml	½ pint	1¼ cups
Poppy seeds	1 tbsp	1 tbsp	1 tbsp

1 Heat the oil in a large frying pan (skillet) or wok and stir-fry all the vegetables, except the mushrooms. Cook for about 10 minutes or until they are just beginning to soften. Add the mushrooms and continue cooking for a further 1–2 minutes.
2 Mix the tomato purée, vinegar, miso and stock or water and stir into the vegetables. Heat through, then stir in the poppy seeds. Serve as a side dish with meat or poultry or as a main course with brown rice or pasta.

NOTE
This is one of the most versatile of dishes because any odd vegetables lying at the bottom of the fridge can be used. As vegetables lose a lot of their vitamin and mineral content with keeping, I've added the miso to compensate as well as to add protein.

SOYA AND SESAME WITH GINGER ROOT SAUCE

This dish is typical of the food eaten by London Olympiad Katie Fitzgibbon, who ran for Britain in the World Cross Country Championships in 1987. She follows the principles of the macrobiotic diet based on grains, a mode of eating which must have proved useful when she ran an ultra across the Himalayas, and the gruelling 42-mile Davos Marathon in Switzerland. Tofu is ideally suited to long-distance runners because it contains no fat and is easily and quickly digested.

Serves 2	Metric	Imperial	American
Tahini	2 tbsp	2 tbsp	2 tbsp
Miso (barley)	1 tbsp	1 tbsp	1 tbsp
Apple juice concentrate	1 tbsp	1 tbsp	1 tbsp
Water	300 ml	½ pint	1¼ cups
Peeled and grated fresh root ginger	1 tsp	1 tsp	1 tsp
Sesame (benne) oil	1 tbsp	1 tbsp	1 tbsp
Firm tofu or tempei	100 g	4 oz	¼ lb
Onions, cut into wedges	2	2	2
Carrots, cut into thin sticks	2	2	2
Courgette (zucchini), sliced	1	1	1
Mushrooms, sliced	50 g	2 oz	½ cup

1 In a saucepan, blend the tahini, miso and apple juice with the water, adding more water if necessary to produce a sauce-like consistency. Stir in the ginger and heat very gently.
2 Meanwhile, heat the oil in a frying pan (skillet) or wok and gently fry the tofu or tempei until browned. Remove from the pan and keep warm. Add the vegetables to the pan and stir-fry until just tender.
3 Transfer the vegetables to a warmed serving dish and place the tofu or tempei on top. Pour the sauce over and serve with brown rice.

STIR-FRY VEGGIES

These stir-fried veggies can be on the table within minutes of your return from a run if you prepare the vegetables before you leave. The accompanying rice can be cooked while you're having your shower.

Serves 4	Metric	Imperial	American
Sunflower oil	*2 tbsp*	*2 tbsp*	*2 tbsp*
Bean sprouts	*225 g*	*8 oz*	*4 cups*
Onion, chopped	*1*	*1*	*1*
Garlic clove, crushed	*1*	*1*	*1*
Carrots, cut into thin strips	*2*	*2*	*2*
Shredded red cabbage	*100 g*	*4 oz*	*1½*
Sliced mushrooms	*100 g*	*4 oz*	*1 cup*
Green pepper, deseeded and sliced	*1*	*1*	*1*
Red pepper, deseeded and sliced	*1*	*1*	*1*
Pumpkin seeds	*50 g*	*2 oz*	*½ cup*
Shoyu	*1 tbsp*	*1 tbsp*	*1 tbsp*

1 Heat the oil in a large frying pan (skillet) or wok. Add all the vegetables and stir-fry for about 10 minutes or until just tender.
2 Quickly stir in the pumpkin seeds and shoyu and serve at once with brown rice.

TOFU, PEPPER AND AUBERGINE BAKE

Serves 4	Metric	Imperial	American
Sunflower oil	*2 tbsp*	*2 tbsp*	*2 tbsp*
Onion, chopped	*1*	*1*	*1*
Green pepper, deseeded and chopped	*½*	*½*	*½*

Red pepper, deseeded and chopped	½	½	½
Medium aubergine (eggplant), chopped	1	1	1
Carrots, finely sliced	2	2	2
Small cooking (tart) apple, cored and chopped	1	1	1
Sultanas (golden raisins)	50 g	2 oz	⅓ cup
Firm tofu, cubed	300 g	10 oz	10 oz
Unsalted peanuts	50 g	2 oz	¼ cup
Ground cumin	1 tsp	1 tsp	1 tsp
Ground coriander	1 tsp	1 tsp	1 tsp
Paprika	1 tsp	1 tsp	1 tsp
Garam masala	1 tsp	1 tsp	1 tsp
Peeled and grated fresh root ginger	½ tsp	½ tsp	½ tsp
Free-range eggs	2	2	2
Skimmed milk	150 ml	¼ pint	⅔ cup

1 Heat the oil in a frying pan (skillet) or wok and sauté the onion for about 5 minutes or until transparent. Add all the vegetables and the apple to the pan and stir-fry for 10 minutes or until soft.
2 Stir in the sultanas, tofu and peanuts with the spices. Continue to cook for a further 2–3 minutes, then turn into a casserole.
3 Beat the eggs and milk together and pour over the top of the vegetables. Bake in a preheated oven at 190°C/375°F (Gas Mark 5) for about 20 minutes or until brown and bubbling.

NUTRITION NOTE
Tofu is a high-protein, non-animal food containing no cholesterol.

LESLEY'S ULTRA VEGETABLE CASSEROLE

Lesley Watson doesn't have time for gourmet cooking with all the international marathons to train for. Her personal best of 2 hours 42 minutes makes her a force to be reckoned with in any race. But the ultra is where she really excels — she currently holds the world record for 50-mile track running.

Serves 4	Metric	Imperial	American
Vegetable margarine	25 g	1 oz	2 tbsp
Potatoes, quartered	450 g	1 lb	1 lb
Carrots, sliced	450 g	1 lb	1 lb
Onions, sliced	3	3	3
Celery stalks, sliced	2	2	2
Small cauliflower, broken into florets	1	1	1
Green pepper, deseeded and cut into strips	1	1	1
Button mushrooms, wiped	225 g	8 oz	2 cups
Tomato purée (paste)	1 tbsp	1 tbsp	1 tbsp
Vegetable stock	600 ml	1 pint	2½ cups
Bay leaf	1	1	1
Freshly ground black pepper			
Potato flour	2 tsp	2 tsp	2 tsp

1 Melt the margarine in a large frying pan (skillet) and sauté all the vegetables for 2–3 minutes. Transfer to a large casserole.
2 Mix the tomato purée with the vegetable stock and pour over the vegetables. Add the bay leaf, season to taste with black pepper, cover and cook in a preheated oven at 190°C/375°F (Gas Mark 5) for 45 minutes.
3 Remove the casserole from the oven. Blend the potato flour with a little cold water and stir into the casserole. Return to the oven and cook for a further 15 minutes. Serve with masses of brown rice.

COURGETTE AND SUNFLOWER STIR-FRY

	Metric	Imperial	American
Serves 2			
Olive oil	2 tbsp	2 tbsp	2 tbsp
Onions, sliced	2	2	2
Courgettes (zucchini), sliced	450 g	1 lb	1 lb
Tomato purée (paste)	1 tbsp	1 tbsp	1 tbsp
Water	150 ml	¼ pint	⅔ cup
Garlic cloves, crushed	2	2	2
Dried oregano	1 tsp	1 tsp	1 tsp
Dried basil	1 tsp	1 tsp	1 tsp
Chopped fresh parsley	1 tbsp	1 tbsp	1 tbsp
Tamari or miso	1 tsp	1 tsp	1 tsp
Sunflower seeds	50 g	2 oz	½ cup
Freshly ground black pepper			

1 Heat the oil in a large frying pan (skillet) or wok and sauté the onions and courgettes for about 5 minutes or until just beginning to soften.
2 Blend the tomato purée with the water and stir in the garlic, oregano, basil, parsley and tamari or miso. Pour this sauce into the pan with the sunflower seeds and simmer gently for about 5 minutes or until the courgettes are cooked. Be careful not to allow them to become too soft; they should be quite crunchy.
3 Season to taste with pepper and serve with brown rice or pasta.

NUTRITION NOTE
The small sunflower seed is rich in B complex vitamins as well as iron, calcium, potassium, magnesium, vitamin A and protein, not to mention all the trace elements. This whole dish can be prepared in less time than it takes to boil the rice so there's no excuse for running short on vitamins because you're short on time.

AUBERGINE CASSEROLE

This is one of my favourite standbys. It avoids the use of fat and the aubergines lose nothing by not being fried before cooking. It is very quick to prepare and can be put in the oven before you go for a run, and the cooking completed while you take a shower afterwards.

Serves 2–3	Metric	Imperial	American
Medium aubergines (eggplants)	2	2	2
Medium onions, sliced	2	2	2
Garlic cloves, crushed	2	2	2
400 g/14 oz can tomatoes	1	1	1
Tomato purée (paste)	4 tbsp	4 tbsp	4 tbsp
Vegetable stock or water	300 ml	½ pint	1¼ cups
Ground coriander	1 tsp	1 tsp	1 tsp
Ground cumin	1 tsp	1 tsp	1 tsp
Cumin seeds	1 tsp	1 tsp	1 tsp
Pinch of ground ginger	1	1	1
Paprika	2 tsp	2 tsp	2 tsp
Mozzarella cheese, sliced	175 g	6 oz	6 oz

1 Cut the aubergines into 1 cm/½ inch slices and place in a casserole with the onions and garlic. Pour over the tomatoes with their juice.
2 Dilute the tomato purée with the stock or water and stir in the spices. Pour this mixture over the aubergines and tomatoes. Cover and cook in a preheated oven at 200°C/400°F (Gas Mark 6) for 45 minutes–1 hour.
3 Uncover the casserole and place the sliced cheese over the top. Return to the oven to cook for a further 20–30 minutes or until the cheese is bubbling and the aubergines are cooked. Serve with pasta or baked potatoes.

NUTRITION NOTE
Vegans can omit the cheese and replace it with a crumble topping of wholewheat breadcrumbs, oats and margarine. If you prefer to avoid the high fat content of Mozzarella, use a low-fat alternative such as Edam.

TIFFANY MUSHROOMS

This slightly naughty starter is best saved for special occasions. Maureen Disbrey thought that she deserved it after running her 1 hour 59 minute half marathon. Maureen is 43 years old and has a training mileage of 30 miles.

Serves 2	Metric	Imperial	American
Medium sherry	*175 ml*	*6 fl oz*	*¾ cup*
Button mushrooms, halved	*225 g*	*8 oz*	*2 cups*
Low-fat mayonnaise	*1 tbsp*	*1 tbsp*	*1 tbsp*
Thick-set low-fat plain yoghurt	*3 tbsp*	*3 tbsp*	*3 tbsp*

1 Bring the sherry to the boil in a small saucepan. Add the mushrooms and cook, stirring, for 2 minutes. Drain the mushrooms into a bowl and reserve the liquor.
2 Return the liquor to the saucepan and boil rapidly until reduced to about 2 tbsp. Allow to cool and add to the mayonnaise.
3 Stir the yoghurt into the mayonnaise and toss the mushrooms in this sauce. Serve over shredded Chinese leaves.

'FRUITS' OF THE SEA

Fish is a high-protein food, low in saturated fat and quick to prepare for the runner in a hurry. However, one of the main considerations for eating it should be for its fat content.

Oily fish, such as mackerel, salmon, herrings, sardines, tuna, pilchards and trout, are all rich in a type of fat which helps to regulate the viscosity of the blood. The result is a reduction of cholesterol and fat in the blood which means there is less likelihood of heart disease or stroke. So beneficial is this effect that experts recommend that vegetarians should supplement their diet with fish oil in capsule form. The oil also affords protection against arthritis, a condition every runner wishes to avoid.

The advent of the microwave has meant fish dishes can be rustled up in no time with all the nutrients retained and the minimum of added fat used. But don't automatically ask for cod or haddock, and instead of salt and vinegar cook yours with herbs and spices. The tasteless steamed fish reminiscent of the nursery or sick bay needn't be the only method for creating a healthy fish dish.

Shellfish have consistently appeared on lists of forbidden foods but now it appears they've been given the green light. Researchers can find no link between the high fat content and cholesterol levels. I do know of a number of runners who suffer from allergic reactions to shellfish, and oysters are supposed to have an aphrodisiac effect, so perhaps you'd be wise to treat them as a luxury for times when your training isn't too demanding!

MICROWAVE SAVOURY TROUT

John Hanscomb runs for Ranelagh Harriers and puts his fitness (he ran his first marathon 32 years ago) down to healthy eating. Whilst many of his training partners are loading up on chips at the pub, he dashes home to cook this trout recipe. As he says, he never sees Hugh Jones in the pub.

Serves 1	Metric	Imperial	American
Tomato, skinned and chopped	1	1	1
Chopped fresh parsley	1 tbsp	1 tbsp	1 tbsp
Mushrooms, chopped	2	2	2
Freshly ground black pepper			
Medium trout, cleaned	1	1	1
Butter or vegetable margarine	25 g	1 oz	2 tbsp
Medium potato, scrubbed and sliced	1	1	1

1 Mix the tomato with the parsley, mushrooms and black pepper to taste and use to stuff the trout.
2 Heat a browning dish on HIGH for 5 minutes or according to the manufacturer's instructions. Add the butter or margarine to the dish and microwave on HIGH for 30 seconds.
3 Place the trout and potato in the browning dish and microwave on HIGH for 6–8 minutes depending on size.
4 Serve with salad or seasonal vegetables.

HERRINGS IN OATMEAL

Serves 2	Metric	Imperial	American
Medium herrings, cleaned	2	2	2
Lemon juice	2 tbsp	2 tbsp	2 tbsp
Freshly ground black pepper			
Fine oatmeal	1 tbsp	1 tbsp	1 tbsp
Sunflower oil	1 tbsp	1 tbsp	1 tbsp
French (Dijon) mustard	1 tbsp	1 tbsp	1 tbsp
Jumbo oats	3 tbsp	3 tbsp	3 tbsp

1 Season the fish inside and out with the lemon juice and black pepper to taste.
2 Coat the fish in the fine oatmeal, brush with the oil and grill (broil) for 3 minutes on each side.
3 Spread each fish with mustard and roll in the oats. Grill for approximately 3 minutes more or until cooked.
4 Serve with grilled mushrooms and wholewheat bread.

FISH AND POTATO BAKE

Serves 4	Metric	Imperial	American
Vegetable oil			
Large onions, chopped	*3*	*3*	*3*
Garlic clove, crushed	*1*	*1*	*1*
Potatoes, scrubbed and sliced	*1 kg*	*2½ lb*	*2½ lb*
Pinch of dried rosemary	*1*	*1*	*1*
Canned mackerel or tuna,			
drained and flaked	*225 g*	*8 oz*	*½ lb*
Vegetable margarine	*50 g*	*2 oz*	*¼ cup*
Skimmed milk	*300 ml*	*½ pint*	*1¼ cups*
Wholewheat breadcrumbs	*50 g*	*2 oz*	*1 cup*
Tomatoes, sliced	*2*	*2*	*2*

1 Heat a little oil in a frying pan (skillet) and sauté the onions and garlic for about 5 minutes or until soft.
2 Lightly grease a large casserole and place a layer of potato and fried onion and garlic in the bottom. Mix the rosemary with the fish and place a layer on top of the potatoes. Continue making alternate layers of potato, onion and fish until all the ingredients are used up, ending with a layer of potato.
3 Dot the potato with margarine and pour over the milk. Sprinkle with breadcrumbs and arrange the tomato slices on top. Bake in a preheated oven at 200°C/400°F (Gas Mark 6) for 1 hour.

NUTRITION NOTE
Mackerel and tuna are good sources of oil containing polyunsaturated fatty acids.

TROUT ALBERT

Albert Kerhoum was raised in France which explains, but doesn't excuse, the cream in this dish. Those with a conscience may substitute plain yoghurt, although the occasional indulgence won't do you any harm. Albert has broken the 3 hour barrier for the marathon, in spite of his indulgences, and regularly runs 40–50 miles per week.

Serves 4	Metric	Imperial	American
Fresh trout, cleaned	4	4	4
Freshly ground black pepper			
Button mushrooms	225 g	8 oz	2 cups
Single (light) cream	150 ml	¼ pint	⅔ cup
Vegetable margarine	40 g	1½ oz	3 tbsp
Sage and onion stuffing mix	50 g	2 oz	2 oz

1 Wash and dry the fish, sprinkle with black pepper and place in an ovenproof dish. Cover and bake at 200°C/400°F (Gas Mark 6) for about 20 minutes.
2 Meanwhile, wipe and slice the mushrooms. Place them in a small saucepan with the cream and simmer gently for 3–4 minutes.
3 Melt the margarine in another pan and stir in the stuffing mix.
4 Remove the fish from the oven and pour over the cream and mushrooms. Sprinkle over the stuffing mixture and return, uncovered, to the oven for a further 5–10 minutes or until the fish is tender.
5 Serve with jacket potatoes and spinach.

MACKEREL WITH APPLE

Serves 4	Metric	Imperial	American
Medium mackerel, cleaned	4	4	4
Wholewheat breadcrumbs	100 g	4 oz	2 cups
Eating apple, cored and			
* roughly chopped*	1	1	1
Fine oatmeal	1 tbsp	1 tbsp	1 tbsp
Grated rind and juice of			
* 1 lemon*			
Chopped fresh parsley	1 tbsp	1 tbsp	1 tbsp
Freshly ground black pepper			
Olive oil			

1 Wash and dry the fish. Combine the breadcrumbs, apple, oatmeal, lemon rind and juice and parsley, and season to taste with black pepper. Use this mixture to stuff the fish.
2 Place the fish in an ovenproof dish and pour a little olive oil over each one. Cover with foil and bake at 190°C/375°F (Gas Mark 5) for 15–20 minutes or until tender.
3 Serve with a seasonal vegetable and potatoes.

NUTRITION NOTE
Mackerel is a nutritious fish rich in essential oils. These oils are thought to be an important protection against arthritis, a disease which worries middle-aged runners.

HADDOCK WITH WALNUT CRUNCH

Serves 4	Metric	Imperial	American
Sunflower oil	2 tbsp	2 tbsp	2 tbsp
Garlic cloves, crushed	2	2	2
Wholewheat breadcrumbs	225 g	8 oz	2 cups
Wheatgerm	25 g	1 oz	¼ cup
Grated rind and juice of 1 orange			
Chopped fresh parsley	1 tbsp	1 tbsp	1 tbsp
Chopped walnuts	50 g	2 oz	½ cup
Haddock or cod steaks	4	4	4
Freshly ground black pepper			

1 Heat the oil in a saucepan and stir in the garlic, breadcrumbs, wheatgerm, orange rind, parsley and walnuts. Heat gently for 2–3 minutes, stirring, until the crumbs are evenly coated with oil.
2 Place the fish in a greased ovenproof dish, season with pepper and pour over the orange juice.
3 Spread the walnut topping over the fish, cover and bake in a preheated oven at 190°C/375°F (Gas Mark 5) for 25 minutes.
4 Serve with large baked potatoes and spinach.

NUTRITION NOTE
The crunchy topping contains extra vitamins E and B complex hidden in the wheatgerm.

SALMON AND BROCCOLI CRUMBLE

Serves 2	Metric	Imperial	American
Sunflower oil	1 tbsp	1 tbsp	1 tbsp
Onion, chopped	1	1	1
Garlic cloves, crushed	2	2	2
Tomatoes, sliced	225 g	8 oz	½ lb
Broccoli	300 g	10 oz	10 oz
Tomato purée (paste)	3 tbsp	3 tbsp	3 tbsp
Water	5 tbsp	5 tbsp	5 tbsp
Freshly ground black pepper			
Dried basil	1 tsp	1 tsp	1 tsp
Small can of salmon, drained and flaked	1	1	1

For the crumble topping

	Metric	Imperial	American
Rolled oats	50 g	2 oz	½ cup
Wheatgerm	25 g	1 oz	¼ cup
Sunflower seeds	1 tbsp	1 tbsp	1 tbsp
Vegetable margarine	50 g	2 oz	¼ cup
Grated Cheddar cheese	50 g	2 oz	½ cup

1 Heat the oil in a large frying pan (skillet) or wok and stir-fry the vegetables for about 10 minutes or until almost tender.
2 Mix the tomato purée with the water, season with pepper and basil and pour on to the vegetables. Cook gently for a further 5 minutes or until the broccoli is tender.
3 Stir the salmon into the vegetable mixture and spoon into an ovenproof dish. Mix all the crumble ingredients together and spoon over the top.
4 Bake in a preheated oven at 190°C/375°F (Gas Mark 5) for 15 minutes or until browned.

VARIATION
Vegetarians may substitute chopped nuts for the fish in this dish, but should consider taking a fish oil supplement.

SWEET AND SOUR PRAWNS

I received this recipe from an anonymous London runner. His personal bests are extremely impressive — 33 minutes for 10K, 56 minutes for 10 miles and a 74 minute half marathon — so I can't understand why he's so modest. I can only assume he's ashamed of the sugar in his favourite dish but I've included it anyway as it tastes so delicious.

Serves 2–3	Metric	Imperial	American
Shoyu or tamari	2 tbsp	2 tbsp	2 tbsp
Vegetable oil	4 tbsp	4 tbsp	4 tbsp
Brown sugar	2 tbsp	2 tbsp	2 tbsp
Wine vinegar	2 tbsp	2 tbsp	2 tbsp
Ground ginger	½ tsp	½ tsp	½ tsp
or			
Peeled and grated fresh root ginger	1 tsp	1 tsp	1 tsp
Freshly ground black pepper			
Large green pepper, deseeded and sliced	1	1	1
Large prawns (shrimp)	350 g	12 oz	¾ lb
Pinch of cayenne pepper	1	1	1
Cornflour (cornstarch)	2 tbsp	2 tbsp	2 tbsp
Water	6 tbsp	6 tbsp	6 tbsp

1 In a large saucepan, mix the shoyu or tamari, half the oil, the sugar, wine vinegar, ginger and black pepper to taste. Bring to the boil, stirring constantly, then reduce the heat to simmer.
2 Meanwhile, heat the remaining oil in a frying pan (skillet) and stir-fry the green pepper for 3–4 minutes or until just soft. Add the prawns and cayenne and continue cooking for a further 2 minutes.
3 Blend the cornflour with the water to make a paste and pour into the sauce with the prawns and pepper. Heat through, stirring, until it thickens.
4 Serve hot with brown rice and a raw vegetable salad.

THE ANIMAL KINGDOM

So you've heard all the arguments, weighed up the pros and cons and you still can't face the week without that visit to the butcher. Endless demands from poorer countries will continue and you will still run the risk of tummy upsets from poorly handled foods and meat loaded with hormones and antibiotics.

I know — meat is a good source of protein and vitamins, particularly B complex, and minerals, but it's important to realise that all these can be found in the vegetable kingdom. You won't suddenly shrink, slow down or become anaemic without your pound of flesh. Nor will the planet become overrun with cattle or sheep if you see the error of your ways.

Cholesterol is the runner's greatest enemy. It's no use having a healthy pair of lungs if the arteries are blocked with fat. The recommended weekly fat intake is 30 per cent and most people will find that fairly restrictive if they eat meat on a daily basis. The following are important guidelines for all flesh eaters:

1 Restrict your meat consumption to 3–4 times per week.
2 Eat less red meat.
3 Choose lean cuts and remove all visible fat.
4 Grill (broil) rather than fry (sauté) and strain off excess melted fat.
5 Add extra carbohydrates to stews and casseroles, e.g. beans, pasta, etc.
6 Buy organically raised poultry.

We all need *some* cholesterol — it's responsible for our sex drive — but all that fat isn't going to turn you into a Mata Hari or Don Juan no matter how much you eat!

BEEF AND BEAN CASSEROLE

Geoffrey Harrington is a Director of Planning at the British Meat Marketing Board and recommends this dish to runners as a low-fat, high-carbohydrate meal. In between warding off the growing vegetarian lobby he averages 25 miles per week. His best half marathon time is 1 hour 39 minutes which is good going for a man in his late fifties who eats meat!

Serves 3–4	Metric	Imperial	American
Lean beef, diced	450 g	1 lb	1 lb
Medium onion, sliced	1	1	1
400 g/14 oz can red kidney beans, drained	1	1	1
225 g/8 oz can baked beans in tomato sauce	1	1	1
Beef stock	300 ml	½ pint	1¼ cups
Chilli powder	1 tsp	1 tsp	1 tsp
Cornflour (cornstarch)	1 tbsp	1 tbsp	1 tbsp
Water	2 tbsp	2 tbsp	2 tbsp

1 Put the beef, onion, red kidney beans, baked beans, beef stock and chilli powder in a casserole. Stir well, cover and cook in the centre of a preheated oven at 160°C/325°F (Gas Mark 3) for about 1½ hours. (This leaves plenty of time for a long run!)
2 Blend the cornflour to a paste with the water. Remove the casserole from the oven and stir the paste into the stew. Return it to the oven to cook for a further 30 minutes. Serve with baked potatoes and green vegetables or, alternatively, brown rice and salad.

POTATO, SPINACH AND BEEF BAKE

Serves 4	Metric	Imperial	American
Lean minced (ground) beef	450 g	1 lb	1 lb
Onion, chopped	1	1	1
300 g/10 oz packet frozen spinach	1	1	1
Dried oregano	1 tsp	1 tsp	1 tsp
Chilli powder (optional)	½ tsp	½ tsp	½ tsp
Grated Parmesan cheese	50 g	2 oz	½ cup
Potatoes, scrubbed and sliced	700 g	1½ lb	1½ lb
400 g/14 oz can tomatoes	1	1	1
Tomato purée (paste)	2 tbsp	2 tbsp	2 tbsp
Hazelnuts, chopped	100 g	4 oz	¾ cup
Rolled oats	100 g	4 oz	1 cup
Sunflower oil	4 tbsp	4 tbsp	4 tbsp
Freshly ground black pepper			

1 Heat a large frying pan (skillet) or wok and sauté the beef, without added fat, until browned. Add the onion, spinach, oregano, chilli, if using, and Parmesan cheese. Cover and cook gently until heated through.
2 Meanwhile, arrange a layer of potato slices in a large ovenproof dish. When the beef and spinach are hot, spoon a layer over the potatoes. Continue to layer beef and potatoes, ending with a layer of potatoes.
3 Combine the tomatoes with their juice and the tomato purée and pour over the casserole.
4 Mix together the hazelnuts, oats, oil and black pepper to taste and arrange over the casserole. Cook in the centre of a preheated oven at 190°C/375°F (Gas Mark 5) for about 1 hour or until the potatoes are cooked. Serve with green vegetables.

NUTRITION NOTE
Spinach is purported to have a laxative effect, so don't eat too much of this the night before an important race!

RON HILL'S LIVER STROGANOFF

Ron is a prolific marathon runner and holder of gold medals in both European (1969) and Commonwealth (1970) Marathons. He has held world records at 10 miles, 15 miles and 25 kilometres and is still the only Briton to have won the Boston Marathon. In 1988 he achieved a personal ambition to run marathons in 50 countries before the age of 50 years. Obviously these are some of the rewards for training for 24 years without missing a day. Or, there again, it could have a lot to do with diet. He recommends eating this recipe once a fortnight for the iron and vitamin B content in the liver.

Serves 2	Metric	Imperial	American
Lamb's liver, sliced	*225 g*	*8 oz*	*½ lb*
Seasoned flour	*2 tbsp*	*2 tbsp*	*2 tbsp*
Vegetable margarine	*40 g*	*1½ oz*	*3 tbsp*
Onion, chopped	*½*	*½*	*½*
Sliced mushrooms	*50 g*	*2 oz*	*½ cup*
Chicken stock	*150 ml*	*¼ pint*	*⅔ cup*
Single (light) cream	*50 ml*	*2 fl oz*	*¼ cup*
Chopped chives, to garnish			

1 Coat the liver in half the seasoned flour. Melt half the margarine in a frying pan (skillet) and sauté the liver for about 5 minutes or until browned. Remove from the pan and set aside.
2 Melt the remaining margarine in the pan and sauté the onion for about 5 minutes or until transparent. Add the mushrooms and stir-fry until soft. Stir in the remaining seasoned flour and cook for 2 minutes, stirring. Gradually pour on the stock and bring to the boil, stirring constantly.
3 Return the liver to the pan and cook for 5 minutes. Stir in the cream and reheat without boiling.
4 Serve on a bed of brown rice, garnished with chives.

LEEK AND LAMB CASSEROLE

Mavis Tomlins from Glasgow enjoys her regular Sunday run knowing the family will be able to enjoy this casserole within an hour of her return. Molasses is one of the best sources of iron and B vitamins so essential for women on the run.

Serves 4	Metric	Imperial	American
Lean lamb	700 g	1½ lb	1½ lb
Vegetable oil	3 tbsp	3 tbsp	3 tbsp
Onions, sliced	2	2	2
Leeks, sliced	2	2	2
Garlic cloves, crushed	2	2	2
400 g/14 oz can tomatoes	1	1	1
Tomato purée (paste)	2 tbsp	2 tbsp	2 tbsp
Ground cinnamon	½ tsp	½ tsp	½ tsp
Cloves	2	2	2
Molasses	1 tsp	1 tsp	1 tsp
Bay leaf	1	1	1
Vegetable stock	450 ml	¾ pint	2 cups
Wholewheat pasta	225 g	8 oz	½ lb
Shelled peas	100 g	4 oz	¾ cup
Freshly ground black pepper			
Chopped fresh parsley	2 tbsp	2 tbsp	2 tbsp

1 Cut the lamb into small cubes, trimming off visible fat.
2 Heat the oil in a heavy saucepan and sauté the onions and leeks for 5–10 minutes or until soft. Add the garlic and lamb and stir-fry until the lamb is evenly browned.
3 Mix the tomatoes with their juice, tomato purée, cinnamon, cloves and molasses and pour over the meat. Bring almost to the boil before transferring to an ovenproof dish. Add the bay leaf, cover and cook in the centre of a preheated oven at 180°C/350°F (Gas Mark 4) for 1 hour.
4 Stir the stock into the casserole with the pasta, peas and black pepper to taste. Return to the oven for another 45 minutes or until the lamb is tender.
5 Serve sprinkled with chopped parsley and accompanied by fresh vegetables and crusty bread.

LAMB AND GRAIN GOULASH

Serves 4	Metric	Imperial	American
Lean lamb	*450 g*	*1 lb*	*1 lb*
Sunflower oil	*2 tbsp*	*2 tbsp*	*2 tbsp*
Medium onions, sliced	*3*	*3*	*3*
Garlic cloves, crushed	*2*	*2*	*2*
Ground coriander	*2 tsp*	*2 tsp*	*2 tsp*
Chilli powder (optional)	*½ tsp*	*½ tsp*	*½ tsp*
Peeled and grated fresh root			
ginger	*2 tsp*	*2 tsp*	*2 tsp*
400 g/14 oz can tomatoes	*1*	*1*	*1*
Bay leaf	*1*	*1*	*1*
Whole wheat grains, soaked			
overnight	*225 g*	*8 oz*	*1¾ cups*
Plain yoghurt	*150 ml*	*¼ pint*	*⅔ cup*
Water or vegetable stock	*300 ml*	*½ pint*	*1¼ cups*
Red wine (optional)	*150 ml*	*¼ pint*	*⅔ cup*
Freshly ground black pepper			

1 Cut the lamb into cubes, removing any visible fat. Heat the oil in a flameproof casserole (Dutch oven) and sauté the onions for about 5 minutes or until transparent. Add the garlic, coriander, chilli if using, ginger and lamb and stir-fry for about 5 minutes or until the meat is browned all over and 'sealed'.

2 Pour the canned tomatoes into the casserole with their juice, add the bay leaf and simmer, uncovered, for 30 minutes or until most of the liquid has been absorbed.

3 Meanwhile, cook the wheat grains in boiling water for about 30 minutes or until soft.

4 Stir the yoghurt into the lamb mixture and continue to simmer until this too has been absorbed. Pour in the water or stock and red wine, if using. Drain the wheat and add to the casserole. Season to taste with black pepper.

5 Cover the casserole and cook in a preheated oven at 170°C/325°F (Gas Mark 3) for about 30 minutes or until the meat is tender. Add more water or stock if the

goulash becomes too dry, although this is not a dish
with a lot of sauce. Serve with boiled potatoes and salad.

NUTRITION NOTE
The whole wheat adds extra flavour, carbohydrate and
B vitamins as well as exercising the jaw! After all, it's
no good running personal bests if you can't talk about
them too!

WHOLESOME HAMBURGERS

Makes 4	Metric	Imperial	American
Lean minced (ground) beef	225 g	8 oz	½ lb
Large potato, grated	1	1	1
Onion, chopped	1	1	1
Chopped fresh parsley	1 tbsp	1 tbsp	1 tbsp
Mixed dried herbs	1 tsp	1 tsp	1 tsp
Freshly ground black pepper			
Tabasco (hot pepper) sauce	½ tsp	½ tsp	½ tsp
Free-range egg, beaten	1	1	1
Wholewheat breadcrumbs, to coat			

1 Mix together the beef, potato and onion. Stir in the
  herbs, pepper to taste and Tabasco. Add the beaten egg
  and form into four burgers.
2 Coat the burgers with wholewheat breadcrumbs and
  cook under the grill (broiler) for about 5 minutes each
  side, or according to taste.
3 Serve in a large wholewheat roll with onions and salad.

NUTRITION NOTE
The potato and roll both help to boost the carbo content of
this meal.

HAM AND NOODLE CASSEROLE

This is a favourite recipe from Sue Tulloh, wife of the famous bare-footed runner Bruce Tulloh. As well as running internationally for nine consecutive years, setting many British and European records, Bruce ran across America from Los Angeles to New York in 65 days. Sue obviously realised that the most important factor affecting athletic performance was not diet but the choice of parents. The Tulloh off-spring are fulfilling their potential with twins Jo and Katy regularly winning races, and son Clive pursuing a sport scholarship in America. Bruce now teaches and coaches at Marlborough School in England where the cross country team is lucky enough to savour the delights of Sue's cooking. There's never a morsel left of this ham and noodle casserole.

Serves 6	Metric	Imperial	American
Wholewheat noodles	225 g	8 oz	½ lb
Vegetable margarine	50 g	2 oz	¼ cup
Medium onion, chopped	1	1	1
Medium green pepper, deseeded and chopped	1	1	1
Mushrooms	225 g	8 oz	½ lb
Thinly sliced cooked ham, cubed	450 g	1 lb	1 lb
Cheddar cheese, grated	225 g	8 oz	½ lb
Canned or fresh tomatoes	350 g	12 oz	¾ lb
Sour cream	600 ml	1 pint	2½ cups
Stoned (pitted) black olives, halved	50 g	2 oz	⅓ cup
Freshly ground black pepper			

1 Cook the noodles in plenty of boiling water for about 8–10 minutes or until just tender. Drain and cool.
2 Melt the margarine in a large saucepan and sauté the onion and green pepper for 3–4 minutes. Slice or halve the mushrooms, depending on size, and add to the pan. Continue to cook for a further 2 minutes.

3   Add all the remaining ingredients to the pan, stir
    thoroughly and mix with the noodles. Transfer the
    mixture to a greased casserole and bake in a preheated
    oven at 180°C/350°F (Gas Mark 4) for 35–40 minutes.
    Serve with French bread and a large salad.

LENTIL AND CHICKEN ROAST

Jill Southgate, a 30 miles per week runner from Norwich,
devised this recipe. The lentils provide extra fibre which
helps to keep runners regular!

Serves 4	Metric	Imperial	American
Lentils	175 g	6 oz	¾ cup
Garlic cloves, crushed	2	2	2
Onions, chopped	2	2	2
Dried sage	2 tsp	2 tsp	2 tsp
Plain yoghurt	150 ml	¼ pint	⅔ cup
Cooked chicken, chopped	225 g	8 oz	½ lb
Red pepper, deseeded and chopped	½	½	½
Free-range egg, beaten	1	1	1
Grated Cheddar cheese	100 g	4 oz	1 cup
Wholewheat breadcrumbs	50 g	2 oz	1 cup
Freshly ground black pepper			

1   Cook the lentils in boiling water for about 25 minutes or
    until soft. Drain well.
2   Mix all the other ingredients together, adding black
    pepper to taste, and stir in the lentils.
3   Press the mixture into a greased and lined 450 g/1 lb loaf
    tin (pan) and bake in a preheated oven at 180°C/350°F
    (Gas Mark 4) for 55 minutes.
4   Turn out and serve in slices with a tomato sauce,
    seasonal vegetables and boiled potatoes.

SPICY CHICKEN CURRY

This is the favourite recipe of Bill Jordan, owner of the famous Jordan's Crunchy Bar empire. He and his family of millers have been promoting the use of whole grains and a healthy lifestyle for years. Bill's personal running achievements are living proof that it works — 2 hours 39 minutes for the marathon, and he completed the London to Paris Triathlon.

Serves 6	Metric	Imperial	American
Vegetable oil	2 tbsp	2 tbsp	2 tbsp
Coriander seeds	1 tsp	1 tsp	1 tsp
Cumin seeds	1 tsp	1 tsp	1 tsp
Onion, chopped	1	1	1
Garlic cloves, crushed	2	2	2
Chicken, jointed	1	1	1
or			
Chicken breasts	6	6	6
Cardamom seeds	10	10	10
Peeled and grated fresh root			
ginger	½ tsp	½ tsp	½ tsp
Garam masala	4 tsp	4 tsp	4 tsp
Ground turmeric	½ tsp	½ tsp	½ tsp
Ground fenugreek	1 tsp	1 tsp	1 tsp
400 g/14 oz can tomatoes	1	1	1
Chicken stock	150 ml	¼ pint	⅔ cup

1 Heat the oil in a large saucepan and fry the coriander and cumin seeds for 2 minutes. Add the onion and garlic and cook for about 5 minutes or until transparent.
2 Add the chicken pieces to the pan and stir-fry until evenly browned. Stir in the remaining spices, reduce the heat and cook for 2 minutes.
3 Pour in the tomatoes with their juice and the stock, cover and simmer for 40 minutes or until the chicken is tender.
4 Serve with brown rice (but preferably not the night before a race)!

LEMON CHICKEN WITH VEGETABLES

This is the sort of dish best reserved for the occasional indulgence — perhaps to celebrate achieving a personal best! Maurice Sampson's hobby is gourmet cooking which does have its side effects — he's often carrying 89 kg (14 stone/196 pounds) on his 1.7 metre (5 foot 7 inch) frame. However, when he left the sugar and fat out, he achieved a 39 minute 39 second 10K, and a body weight of 69 kg (10 stone 12 pounds/ 152 pounds).

Serves 4	Metric	Imperial	American
Large chicken breast fillets, skinned	4	4	4
Paprika	2 tbsp	2 tbsp	2 tbsp
Medium courgettes (zucchini), sliced	5	5	5
Large onion, sliced	1	1	1
Garlic cloves, crushed	8	8	8
Dried oregano	1 tbsp	1 tbsp	1 tbsp
Unsalted butter	150 g	5 oz	10 tbsp
Lemon juice	4 tbsp	4 tbsp	4 tbsp
Medium carrots, sliced	4	4	4
Medium potatoes, quartered	6	6	6
Freshly ground black pepper			
Mushrooms, sliced	175 g	6 oz	1½ cups

1 Place the chicken in a large casserole and sprinkle with the paprika. Arrange the courgettes around the chicken.
2 Place half the onion, garlic and oregano on top of the courgettes, dot with half the butter, then pour half the lemon juice over. Add the carrots and potatoes, followed by the remaining oregano, garlic, lemon juice and butter.
3 Season the casserole with pepper to taste and cover with a tight-fitting lid. Cook in a preheated oven at 200°C/400°F (Gas Mark 6) for 40 minutes.
4 Remove the casserole from the oven and add the remaining onion and all the mushrooms. Re-cover the dish and return to the oven for a further 30 minutes.

MAGGIE'S CHICKEN WITH MANGO

Maggie Moule derives her inspiration for recipes whilst running the streets of London. She races over distances from 10K to marathons with personal bests of 41 minutes and 3 hours 55 minutes respectively. This recipe is convenient because it allows you at least 4 hours to fit in a run while the chicken is marinating.

Serves 2–3	Metric	Imperial	American
Chicken breast fillets, skinned and sliced into strips	350 g	12 oz	¾ lb
Piece of fresh root ginger, peeled and finely chopped	15–25 g	½–1 oz	½–1 oz
Fresh green chillies, deseeded and chopped	2–3	2–3	2–3
Shoyu or tamari	2 tbsp	2 tbsp	2 tbsp
Polyunsaturated oil	4 tbsp	4 tbsp	4 tbsp
Garlic cloves, crushed	2	2	2
Freshly ground black pepper			
Medium mangoes	2	2	2
Chicken stock	2 tbsp	2 tbsp	2 tbsp

1 Place the chicken, ginger and chillies in a bowl and stir in the shoyu or tamari sauce, half the oil, the garlic and black pepper to taste. Cover and place in the refrigerator for at least 4 hours.
2 To prepare the mangoes, peel them and cut thick slices of flesh from each side of the stone, then slice thinly.
3 Heat the remaining oil in a large frying pan (skillet) or wok and stir-fry the chicken for 1–2 minutes. Stir in the stock and cook for a further 3–4 minutes. Finally, stir in the mango and serve at once with brown rice and a green salad.

AUDREY'S CHICKEN CURRY

Audrey Bergstrom started running in her fifties when she married the Chairman of Burnham Joggers. She took on more than she bargained for when she discovered he had a cholesterol problem too. However, this curry is an example of her successful method of reducing his fat intake, whilst allowing herself valuable time for training.

Serves 1 hungry runner or
  2 polite supporters!

	Metric	Imperial	American
Chicken breast fillet, skinned	1	1	1
Curry powder	2 tsp	2 tsp	2 tsp
Pinch of paprika	1	1	1
Pinch of ground turmeric	1	1	1
Pinch of chilli powder	1	1	1
White pepper			
Chicken stock (bouillon) cube	1	1	1
Boiling water	900 ml	1½ pints	3¾ cups
Tomato, chopped	1	1	1
Mushrooms, chopped	6	6	6
Large carrots, diced	2	2	2
Large potatoes, diced	2	2	2
Large onion, sliced	1	1	1
Lentils	100 g	4 oz	½ cup

1 Dice the chicken breast and place in a large saucepan with the curry powder, paprika, turmeric, chilli powder and pepper to taste.
2 Dissolve the stock cube in the boiling water and add to the pan. Cover and bring to the boil. Reduce the heat and simmer very gently for 45 minutes.
3 Add the vegetables and lentils and simmer for about 30 minutes or until the vegetables are tender and the curry nicely thickened, stirring occasionally.
4 Serve with brown rice, sliced cucumber and plain yoghurt.

CHICKEN AND WALNUT PASTA

Serves 4	Metric	Imperial	American
Wholewheat pasta shapes	350 g	12 oz	3 cups
Vegetable oil	2 tbsp	2 tbsp	2 tbsp
Onions, chopped	1	1	1
Chicken breast fillets, skinned	4	4	4
Mushrooms, sliced	175 g	6 oz	1½ cups
Plain wholewheat flour	25 g	1 oz	¼ cup
Chicken stock	300 ml	½ pint	1¼ cups
225 g/8 oz can tomatoes	1	1	1
Tomato purée (paste)	1 tbsp	1 tbsp	1 tbsp
Mustard	1 tsp	1 tsp	1 tsp
Sultanas (golden raisins)	50 g	2 oz	⅓ cup
Walnut pieces	50 g	2 oz	½ cup
Dried thyme	1 tsp	1 tsp	1 tsp
Freshly ground black pepper			

1 Cook the pasta in plenty of boiling water, with 1 tsp oil added, for 8–10 minutes or until tender.

2 Meanwhile, heat the remaining oil in a large frying pan (skillet) or wok and sauté the onion for 3–4 minutes.

3 Cut the chicken into bite-sized pieces and add to the pan. Stir-fry until just beginning to brown. Stir in the mushrooms and cook for a further 3–4 minutes.

4 Sprinkle on the flour and stir until the fat is absorbed.

5 Mix together the stock, tomatoes and juice, tomato purée and mustard and slowly add to the pan, stirring continuously to prevent sticking. Stir in the sultanas, walnuts, thyme and black pepper to taste.

6 Lower the heat and simmer for a further 10 minutes or until the chicken is cooked.

7 Drain the pasta and stir into the chicken mixture. Serve with a large mixed salad.

NUTRITION NOTE
Chicken is probably the healthiest of the animal flesh around but do look for free-range birds. The poor

cage-reared bird is probably pumped full of antibiotics and chemicals which are best avoided.

ITALIAN CHICKEN

Kevin Willis from Gloucester sent me this recipe which he devised on reaching the decision to abandon red meat.

Serves 4	Metric	Imperial	American
Sunflower oil	2 tbsp + 1 tsp	2 tbsp + 1 tsp	2 tbsp + 1 tsp
Large onions, chopped	2	2	2
Small green pepper, deseeded and chopped	1	1	1
Garlic cloves, crushed	2	2	2
Chicken breast fillets, skinned and diced	350 g	12 oz	¾ lb
400 g/14 oz can tomatoes	1	1	1
Tomato purée (paste)	2 tbsp	2 tbsp	2 tbsp
Dried basil	1 tsp	1 tsp	1 tsp
Dried oregano	2 tsp	2 tsp	2 tsp
Freshly ground black pepper			
Wholewheat spaghetti	350 g	12 oz	¾ lb
Grated Parmesan cheese			

1 Heat 2 tbsp sunflower oil in a large frying pan (skillet) or wok and stir-fry the onions and green pepper for 5–10 minutes or until soft. Add the garlic and chicken and stir-fry for a few more minutes or until browned.
2 Mix the tomatoes and juice, tomato purée, herbs and black pepper to taste and pour over the chicken. Cover and simmer gently for 45 minutes, adding a little water if the mixture becomes too dry.
3 Cook the spaghetti in plenty of boiling water, with the extra 1 tsp oil added, for 8–10 minutes or until tender. Drain, divide between warmed serving plates and pour over the chicken sauce. Sprinkle with Parmesan cheese and serve with a large mixed salad.

ZESTY SALADS

Nature's answer to the 'fast food' merchants must be the salad meal. Even those who only enter the kitchen when they smell burning can grate a carrot or chop an apple.

Contrary to popular belief, it isn't necessary to eat all our meals hot. Psychologically, hot food may be a great comfort, especially after winter running, but we could be missing out a lot of goodness. Food subjected to high temperatures often loses its nutrients, many of which are poured down the kitchen sink, destined to nourish only the inhabitants of the drains. Vitamin C disappears after only slight heating, and iron, calcium and potassium may also dissolve in water. Certain enzymes, which aid in the digestion of food, are destroyed above 60°C (140°F). Acne is one of the complaints attributed to the lack of these enzymes. If you've a teenage sprinter in the family, make sure she or he eats a salad daily.

Almost all vegetables can be eaten raw, with the exception of the potato. Add cooked pasta or whole grains and a few nuts, seeds or dried fruit to boost the carbohydrate content. Bean sprouts are incredibly nutritious yet still a mystery food to a lot of runners. They have all the nutrients of the bean but multiplied hundreds of times over.

With the huge variety of fruits and vegetables on the market, it's possible to assemble a different combination for every day without resorting to the ubiquitous lettuce and tomato. Would you believe that there is six times more vitamin C in spinach leaves than in lettuce anyway?

Once you've prepared your salad, don't go and turn it into junk food by ladling on the salad creams. Prepare a low-fat alternative by mixing a small carton of plain yoghurt with 1 tsp lemon juice and a few chopped fresh herbs. Adding a little wheatgerm will increase your B vitamins.

Make a salad meal a daily part of your diet and long-suffering partners may adopt a more tolerant attitude to your running if they aren't expected to devise 101 ways to prevent the gravy drying up!

THE ALTERNATIVE GREEN SALAD

Serves 2	Metric	Imperial	American
Small green cabbage, sliced	¼	¼	¼
Brussels sprouts, sliced	4	4	4
Chopped celery leaves	2 tbsp	2 tbsp	2 tbsp
Spinach leaves, chopped	4	4	4
Broccoli sprigs, broken into florets	2	2	2
Bunch of watercress	1	1	1
Green pepper, deseeded and sliced	½	½	½
Nasturtium leaves (optional)	3–4	3–4	3–4
Chopped fresh mint	1 tbsp	1 tbsp	1 tbsp
Green eating apple, cored and chopped	1	1	1
Olive oil	120 ml	4 fl oz	½ cup
Lemon juice	3 tbsp	3 tbsp	3 tbsp
Cider vinegar	3 tbsp	3 tbsp	3 tbsp
Freshly ground black pepper			
Pumpkin seeds	1 tbsp	1 tbsp	1 tbsp

1 Arrange all the green vegetables, nasturtium leaves if using, mint and apple in a large salad bowl.
2 Beat the oil, lemon juice, vinegar and black pepper to taste together and pour over the salad.
3 Sprinkle over the pumpkin seeds and chill in the refrigerator. Serve with wholewheat bread.

NUTRITION NOTE
This is a marvellous way to stock up on almost all the important vitamins and minerals — not a lettuce leaf in sight and cheaper than all those vitamin pills!

FRUIT AND NUT SALAD

Serves 4–6	Metric	Imperial	American
Shredded white cabbage	100 g	4 oz	¼ lb
Shredded red cabbage	100 g	4 oz	¼ lb
Celery stalks, sliced	4	4	4
Carrots, grated	2	2	2
No-need-to-soak dried apricots	50 g	2 oz	⅓ cup
Chopped stoned (pitted) dates	50 g	2 oz	⅓ cup
Sultanas (golden raisins)	50 g	2 oz	⅓ cup
Eating apples, cored and grated	2	2	2
Chopped mixed nuts	50 g	2 oz	½ cup
Sunflower oil	75 ml	3 fl oz	⅓ cup
Lemon juice	2 tbsp	2 tbsp	2 tbsp
Plain yoghurt	120 ml	4 fl oz	½ cup
Tahini	1 tbsp	1 tbsp	1 tbsp
Sesame (benne) seeds	1 tbsp	1 tbsp	1 tbsp

1 In a large salad bowl, mix together all the vegetables, fruits and nuts.
2 Beat together the oil, lemon juice, yoghurt and tahini until smooth and pour over the salad.
3 Mix the salad well and sprinkle with the sesame seeds. Serve chilled with masses of wholewheat bread.

NUTRITION NOTE
You can keep a bowl of this in the fridge to last over several days. It will keep your supply of vitamins and minerals high, as well as providing extra energy. Take a pot to work to eat with bread and you won't experience that 'energy gap'.

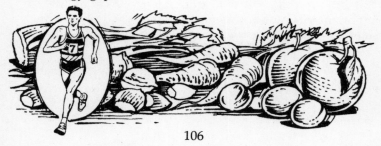

TABOULI

It would be hard to find a more refreshing summer salad.

Serves 4	Metric	Imperial	American
Bulgar wheat	*350 g*	*12 oz*	*¾ lb*
Olive oil	*6 tbsp*	*6 tbsp*	*6 tbsp*
Lemon juice	*2 tbsp*	*2 tbsp*	*2 tbsp*
Vinegar	*2 tbsp*	*2 tbsp*	*2 tbsp*
Garlic clove, crushed	*1*	*1*	*1*
Dijon mustard	*1 tsp*	*1 tsp*	*1 tsp*
Paprika	*1 tsp*	*1 tsp*	*1 tsp*
Tomato, chopped	*1*	*1*	*1*
Onion, chopped	*1*	*1*	*1*
10 cm/4 inch piece of cucumber, diced	*1*	*1*	*1*
Chopped fresh mint	*3 tbsp*	*3 tbsp*	*3 tbsp*
Chopped fresh parsley	*2 tbsp*	*2 tbsp*	*2 tbsp*
Lettuce leaves, to serve			

1 Place the bulgar wheat in a large bowl, and pour in sufficient hot water to cover by 5–7.5 cm/2–3 inches. Leave to hydrate for 30 minutes.
2 Meanwhile, make the dressing by whisking together the oil, lemon juice, vinegar, garlic, mustard and paprika.
3 Drain the bulgar thoroughly. This is most important as the drier the grain is the more flavour it will absorb. The best method is to squeeze it in a piece of muslin (cheesecloth).
4 Stir in the tomato, onion, cucumber, mint and parsley. Pour on the dressing, toss and chill before serving in a bowl lined with lettuce.

ORIENTAL BEAN SPROUTS

Serves 2	Metric	Imperial	American
Sliced spring onions (scallions)	1 tbsp	1 tbsp	1 tbsp
Red pepper, deseeded and diced	½	½	½
Button mushrooms, sliced	2–3	2–3	2–3
Bean sprouts	225 g	8 oz	4 cups
Plain yoghurt	150 ml	¼ pint	⅔ cup
Lemon juice	1 tbsp	1 tbsp	1 tbsp
Small garlic clove, crushed	1	1	1
Low-fat mayonnaise	1 tbsp	1 tbsp	1 tbsp
Tamari or shoyu	1 tsp	1 tsp	1 tsp
Peeled and grated fresh root ginger	1 tsp	1 tsp	1 tsp

1 Mix the vegetables and the bean sprouts in a salad bowl.
2 Combine all the remaining ingredients to make the dressing.
3 Pour the dressing over the salad, toss and chill thoroughly before serving.

NUTRITION NOTE
If you include bean sprouts in your diet you'll never run short of vitamins. They include vitamins A, C, E and B complex as well as minerals and enzymes. Once sprouted, the vitamin content of the beans can increase by as much as 800 per cent.

BUCKWHEAT SALAD

Serves 4	Metric	Imperial	American
Roasted buckwheat	*225 g*	*8 oz*	*½ lb*
Onion, chopped	*1*	*1*	*1*
Large red eating apple, cored			
and chopped	*1*	*1*	*1*
Sultanas (golden raisins)	*50 g*	*2 oz*	*⅓ cup*
Carrot, grated	*1*	*1*	*1*
White wine vinegar	*1 tbsp*	*1 tbsp*	*1 tbsp*
Lemon juice	*2 tbsp*	*2 tbsp*	*2 tbsp*
Sunflower oil	*3 tbsp*	*3 tbsp*	*3 tbsp*
Freshly ground black pepper			
Endive (chicory)	*1*	*1*	*1*

1 Cook the buckwheat in boiling water (2 parts water to
  1 part grain) for about 20 minutes or until tender. Drain
  and stir in the onion, apple, sultanas and carrot.
2 Beat together the vinegar, lemon juice, oil and pepper to
  taste and use to dress the buckwheat.
3 Arrange the endive leaves in a large salad bowl and pile
  the buckwheat in the centre.

NUTRITION NOTE
Buckwheat contains all the essential amino acids, and is
rich in potassium, thiamin and iron. Riboflavin, which is
essential for maintaining good circulation, is also present in
high amounts. The Russians have known the benefits of
this highly nutritional grain for years. It is thought to
control blood pressure — could it be responsible for
Glasnost?!

FRUITY BEAN SALAD

Serves 4	Metric	Imperial	American
Mixed dried beans (red kidney, haricot/navy and chick-peas)	450 g	1 lb	1 lb
Onion, chopped	1	1	1
Garlic clove, crushed	1	1	1
Small green pepper, deseeded and diced	1	1	1
Small red pepper, deseeded and diced	1	1	1
Orange, peeled, segmented and cut into chunks	1	1	1
Slices of fresh pineapple, cubed	2–3	2–3	2–3
Sunflower oil	120 ml	4 fl oz	½ cup
Cider vinegar	2 tbsp	2 tbsp	2 tbsp
Peeled and grated fresh root ginger	1 tsp	1 tsp	1 tsp
Tamari or shoyu	1 tsp	1 tsp	1 tsp
Squeeze of lemon juice	1	1	1
Freshly ground black pepper			

1 Soak the beans in water overnight, then drain and cook
   in boiling water for 1–1½ hours or until tender. Drain
   and set aside to cool.
2 Mix the vegetables and fruit together in a large bowl.
3 Combine the oil, vinegar, ginger, tamari or shoyu, lemon
   juice and black pepper to taste.
4 Place the cooled beans in a large salad bowl and stir in
   the fruits and vegetables. Pour over the dressing and stir
   well to coat evenly. Chill before serving with lots of
   crusty wholewheat bread.

NOTE
Cooked beans freeze well and it's worth steaming up the
kitchen during the winter to provide bags of instant beans
for use during the summer months. If time and space are
short, you can substitute canned beans, but rinse off the
water first because it's usually full of salt and sugar.

SPEEDY CHICKEN SALAD

One runner I know takes a portion of this salad to work with him for lunch. With a couple of fresh rolls bought from the corner baker's shop he has a satisfying and sustaining meal.

Serves 4	Metric	Imperial	American
Plain yoghurt	*4 tbsp*	*4 tbsp*	*4 tbsp*
Dijon mustard	*½ tsp*	*½ tsp*	*½ tsp*
Cooked chicken, diced	*225 g*	*8 oz*	*½ lb*
Spring onions (scallions), sliced	*4*	*4*	*4*
Carrot, diced,	*1*	*1*	*1*
Celery stalks, sliced	*2*	*2*	*2*
Seedless white grapes	*50 g*	*2 oz*	*½ cup*
Sunflower seeds	*1 tbsp*	*1 tbsp*	*1 tbsp*
Chopped fresh parsley	*1 tbsp*	*1 tbsp*	*1 tbsp*

1 Mix the yoghurt and mustard together.
2 Place all the other ingredients, except the parsley, in a large salad bowl, pour on the dressing and stir.
3 Sprinkle the parsley over the top and serve with crusty wholewheat bread.

THREE-GRAIN SALAD BOWL

Serves 4–6	Metric	Imperial	American
Whole wheat grains, soaked overnight and drained	100 g	4 oz	¾ cup
Pot barley	100 g	4 oz	½ cup
Brown rice	100 g	4 oz	½ cup
Red pepper, deseeded and chopped	1	1	1
Cucumber, chopped	½	½	½
Medium onion, chopped	1	1	1
Tomatoes, chopped	2	2	2
Celery stalk, sliced	1	1	1
Raisins	50 g	2 oz	⅓ cup
Chopped fresh parsley	1 tbsp	1 tbsp	1 tbsp
Chopped fresh mint	2 tsp	2 tsp	2 tsp
Sunflower oil	4 tbsp	4 tbsp	4 tbsp
Juice of ½ lemon			

1 Cook the wheat and barley together in plenty of boiling water for about 30 minutes, then stir in the rice and continue cooking for a further 30 minutes or until all the grains are tender. Drain and cool.
2 Tip the grains into a large salad bowl and stir in the vegetables, raisins and herbs.
3 Beat the oil and lemon juice together and pour over the salad. Chill well before serving.

NUTRITION NOTE
This salad is very high in carbohydrate — just the sort of meal you should be eating during marathon training. The crunchy texture of the grains will ensure your jaw doesn't miss out on exercise when you're churning out all those long silent miles.

JUST DESSERTS

Ideally, the committed runner should bypass this section because the only sugar he or she really needs can be obtained from natural sources. Fresh fruit or yoghurt are all that's necessary to round off a meal. However, runners are a notorious breed when it comes to sweetness, and many still see their favourite pudding as a fitting reward after a hard training session.

There isn't anything wrong in the occasional indulgence, as long as you don't make a habit of it. Your day-to-day diet should avoid refined sugars which slow down the passage of food through the gut, which in turn can lead to obesity and constipation. These are two conditions strongly implicated in heart disease and cancer of the bowel.

Brown sugar and honey are potentially as harmful as white sugar but because they're in an unrefined state they do at least provide some fibre and minerals. The very dark muscovado and molasses sugars also taste much stronger so there's always the possibility that you'll use less. A much healthier method of sweetening desserts is to use concentrated fruit juices. Mixed with a little water and poured over fresh fruit they produce a refreshing alternative to canned fruit in syrup.

Be adventurous in your choice of fruit which, nowadays, is almost overwhelming. Supermarket shelves are often brimful of exotic varieties from all over the world. Fruit brings an added bonus for the digestive system because it contains water-soluble fibre. It's this type of fibre which helps to lower cholesterol levels by absorbing harmful saturated fats. We should all aim to eat at least two pieces of fruit a day.

If you're still not convinced and your teeth are false anyway, at least *try* one of the following recipes which are nutritious as well as sweet. But do save it until after you've trained or you'll be dragging your heels for several miles. Remember to add an extra lap to the next run, too, in case that guilty feeling weighs heavy. No matter how many puddings we eat, I'm sure we'll all receive our just desserts in the long run!

CAROB PEARS

Serves 4	Metric	Imperial	American
Ripe pears	4	4	4
Bar of plain carob	1	1	1
Orange juice	1 tsp	1 tsp	1 tsp
Grated rind of 1 orange			
Free-range egg, separated	1	1	1
Sesame (benne) seeds, to			
decorate	1 tbsp	1 tbsp	1 tbsp

1 Peel the pears but leave the stalks intact. Poach the pears in boiling water for about 20 minutes or until just tender. (This can be done quickly by placing the pears in a plastic bag with 1 tbsp water and cooking in a microwave.)
2 Break the bar of carob into pieces and melt in a small saucepan with 1 tbsp water. Allow to cool slightly before stirring in the orange juice, rind and egg yolk. Whisk the egg white until dry and stiff and carefully fold into the carob.
3 Arrange the pears in individual dishes and pour a portion of carob sauce over each. Decorate with the sesame seeds.

NUTRITION NOTE
Carob is a much healthier food than chocolate because it contains no caffeine. Migraine sufferers therefore can enjoy the taste of chocolate without the after-effects.

MARATHONER'S BREAD AND BUTTER PUDDING

Serves 4	Metric	Imperial	American
Slices of Fruit Loaf with Cinnamon	6–8	6–8	6–8
Butter, softened	25 g	1 oz	2 tbsp
Free-range eggs	2	2	2
Skimmed milk	900 ml	1½ pints	3¾ cups
Sugar	15 g	½ oz	1 tbsp
Pure vanilla essence (extract)	2 tsp	2 tsp	2 tsp
Pinch of ground cinnamon	1	1	1
Sultanas (golden raisins)	1 tbsp	1 tbsp	1 tbsp
Raisins	1 tbsp	1 tbsp	1 tbsp

1 Thinly spread the fruit loaf slices with the butter.
2 Beat the eggs into the milk and add the sugar, vanilla essence and cinnamon.
3 Place a layer of bread, buttered side up, in the bottom of a greased ovenproof dish. Sprinkle a few sultanas and raisins over and continue to layer with bread and fruit, ending with a layer of fruit.
4 Slowly pour on three quarters of the milk mixture and bake in a preheated oven at 190°C/375°F (Gas Mark 5) for 30 minutes.
5 Remove the pudding from the oven and pour on the remaining milk. Bake for a further 20 minutes or until nicely browned. Serve on its own or with plain yoghurt.

VARIATION
You could use any of the more unusual grain breads and sprinkle sesame (benne) seeds and oats over the top. Soya milk, although not universally enjoyed on its own, gives a surprisingly creamy taste to cooked dishes.

STRAWBERRY AND TOFU ICE CREAM

Serves 4	Metric	Imperial	American
Tofu	225 g	8 oz	½ lb
Fresh strawberries, hulled	100 g	4 oz	1¼ cups
Wholewheat breadcrumbs	50 g	2 oz	1 cup
Vanilla essence	½ tsp	½ tsp	½ tsp
Brown sugar	40 g	1½ oz	3 tbsp
Vegetable margarine	1½ tbsp	1½ tbsp	1½ tbsp
Sunflower oil	2 tbsp	2 tbsp	2 tbsp
Sherry (optional)	1 tbsp	1 tbsp	1 tbsp
Mint leaves and whole strawberries, to decorate			

1 Place all the ingredients in a blender or food processor and blend until smooth.
2 Spoon the mixture into a small freezer tray and freeze overnight.
3 Remove the ice cream from the freezer 5 minutes before serving. Decorate with mint and strawberries.

VARIATION
This is one of the few ways I know of eating ice cream without feeling guilty. The fruit content can be varied endlessly, but don't leave out the breadcrumbs.

BANANA CREAM

Serves 2–3	Metric	Imperial	American
Cashew nuts	100 g	4 oz	¼ lb
Stoned (pitted) dates	6	6	6
Arrowroot	1 tbsp	1 tbsp	1 tbsp
Vanilla essence	1 tsp	1 tsp	1 tsp
Water	300 ml	½ pint	1¼ cups
Ripe bananas	2	2	2
Caronut or chocolate and nut spread	2 tsp	2 tsp	2 tsp

1 Place all the ingredients, except the bananas and caronut, in a blender or food processor and blend.
2 Transfer to a saucepan and heat gently until the sauce thickens. Stir in the caronut until well blended.
3 Peel and slice the bananas and place in individual dishes. Pour the sauce over the top and serve chilled.

NUTRITION NOTE
Bananas are a good source of carbohydrate as well as potassium. Combined with the nuts and dates, they produce a highly nutritious pudding to provide even the most lethargic with a new zest for life.

RASPBERRY SORBET

Serves 4	Metric	Imperial	American
Fresh or frozen raspberries	450 g	1 lb	1 lb
Low-fat plain yoghurt	150 ml	¼ pint	⅔ cup
Concentrated apple juice	2 tbsp	2 tbsp	2 tbsp
Sultanas (golden raisins)	50 g	2 oz	⅓ cup
Sesame (benne) seeds	25 g	1 oz	¼ cup

1 Put all the ingredients in a blender or food processor and purée until smooth.
2 Pour the purée into a small 18 × 28 cm/7 × 11 inch freezer tray and freeze.
3 When almost frozen, tip the sorbet (sherbet) back into the blender or food processor and re-process until creamy. Either return to the original freezer tray or spoon into the shells of small oranges. Cover with cling film (plastic wrap) and freeze.
4 Remove from the freezer 15 minutes before serving.

NUTRITION NOTE
Raspberries contain more fibre than most other fruits. The sultanas will boost supplies of potassium and carbohydrate, and sesame seeds add extra calcium. In fact, no other food contains as much calcium — even milk can provide only one tenth as much.

APRICOT AND APPLE CRUMBLE

Serves 4	Metric	Imperial	American
Cooking (tart) apples	450 g	1 lb	1 lb
Dried apricots, soaked overnight in fresh orange juice	100 g	4 oz	1/4 lb
Sultanas (golden raisins)	50 g	2 oz	1/3 cup
Concentrated apple juice	200 ml	1/3 pint	7/8 cup
Plain wholewheat flour	175 g	6 oz	1 1/2 cups
Ground cinnamon	1 tsp	1 tsp	1 tsp
Vegetable margarine	75 g	3 oz	1/3 cup
Rolled oats	50 g	2 oz	1/2 cup
Sunflower seeds	25 g	1 oz	1/4 cup

1 Wash and dry the apples and core them, but do not peel. Slice the apples horizontally and place in an ovenproof dish. Arrange the apricots and sultanas over the top and pour on the apple juice.
2 Place the flour and cinnamon in a bowl and rub (cut) in the margarine until the mixture resembles breadcrumbs. Stir in the oats and seeds.
3 Spoon the crumble over the fruit and bake in a preheated oven at 190°C/375°F (Gas Mark 5) for 30 minutes. Serve with Greek or plain yoghurt.

NUTRITION NOTE
The unpeeled apples, oats and sunflower seeds all boost the fibre content of this old English pudding.

TROPICAL FRUIT SALAD

Serves 4	Metric	Imperial	American
Black grapes, deseeded	225 g	8 oz	½ lb
White grapes, deseeded	225 g	8 oz	½ lb
Kiwi fruit, peeled and sliced	2	2	2
Small red eating apples, cored and sliced	4	4	4
Mango, peeled, stoned (pitted) and sliced	1	1	1
Banana, peeled and sliced	1	1	1
Can of lychees, drained and rinsed	1	1	1
Slices of fresh pineapple	4	4	4
Flaked (slivered) almonds	100 g	4 oz	1 cup
Fresh orange juice	300 ml	½ pint	1¼ cups
Lemon juice	1 tsp	1 tsp	1 tsp

1 Mix all the fruits together, except the pineapple, and stir in the almonds.
2 Mix the orange juice and lemon juice together and pour over the fruit. Chill for several hours.
3 Place a slice of pineapple on each of four individual serving plates and spoon the salad over the top.
4 Serve with Greek yoghurt or a low-fat cream, if you must!

NUTRITION NOTE
This is particularly refreshing after a long summer run. The wide variety of fruits will ensure that you quickly replace any vitamins and minerals you may have lost through sweating.

FIGGY PUDDING

Makes 12 portions	Metric	Imperial	American
Free-range eggs, beaten	2	2	2
Vegetable margarine	100 g	4 oz	½ cup
Molasses	150 g	5 oz	½ cup
Runny honey	150 g	5 oz	½ cup
Raisins	50 g	2 oz	⅓ cup
Currants	50 g	2 oz	⅓ cup
Chopped walnuts	50 g	2 oz	½ cup
Plain yoghurt	250 ml	8 fl oz	1 cup
Figs	350 g	12 oz	¾ lb
Small orange, peeled and quartered	1	1	1
Self-raising wholewheat flour	350 g	12 oz	3 cups
Ground cinnamon	1 tsp	1 tsp	1 tsp
Grated nutmeg	½ tsp	½ tsp	½ tsp
Ground allspice	1 tsp	1 tsp	1 tsp

1 Beat the eggs and margarine together and beat in the molasses and honey. Stir in the raisins, currants, nuts and yoghurt.
2 Place the figs and orange pieces in a blender or food processor and blend until smooth.
3 Add the purée to the fruit mixture.
4 Mix the dry ingredients together and fold into the fruit, etc. Spoon into a large baking tin or ring mould and cook in a preheated oven at 160°C/325°F (Gas Mark 3) for 1 hour or until firm to the touch.
5 Serve warm with Greek yoghurt.

FLUID FACTS

We can eat pasta until the cows come home, but on race day we're obsessed with fluids. Runners have searched for many years to find a magic potion, pinning their hopes on some peculiar elixirs. Early marathoners personally distributed their drinks to the feeding stations and their contents were closely guarded secrets. One ingredient common to all was sugar, which meant these pioneers were slowly running up the garden path!

The more sugary the drink, including glucose, the longer the fluid will remain in the stomach, because it is required in the digestive process. During an endurance event, we need the fluid in the muscles and as quickly as possible. You should therefore avoid all sugary drinks before and during long runs, and this includes all fruit juices. Even those un-sweetened varieties contain natural sugars.

Salt was another of the magic constituents often swallowed in an attempt to replace that which was lost through sweat-ing. We do indeed lose salt, but as the body stores at least double our requirements it's not important, unless you train near the equator. Too much salt will cause an imbalance of electrolytes.

A few years ago 'electrolyte' was a buzz word appearing on new sports drinks which claimed to restore their balance. The advertising gave the impression that a tumbler-full be-fore and after running would offset dehydration and improve performance. Sweat does contain electrolytes, but only a small number as it's 99.1 per cent water. What happens is that the remaining electrolytes become more concentrated because of the water loss. If you do experiment with these drinks, remember this fact and add a lot more water than the label advises. There again, you could save yourself some cash and take your water neat.

Coffee has been a pre-race favourite for years and the latest research does indicate it may have a place. A couple of cups taken before endurance events apparently stimulates the release of free fatty acids early in the race. This means that you don't draw on the muscle glycogen until much later. Unfortunately, it doesn't work for everyone, and if you're a caffeine addict anyway, remember that it inhibits the absorption of iron.

More runs have been ruined by dehydration than failure to drink some witch's brew. The human body is 50–60 per cent water and even on a warm day we can lose 1–8 per cent of that. (Women lose more when menstruating.) The practice used to be to drink at regular intervals during the run, but I'm convinced it's even more important to be adequately hydrated before you start. On a hot day, this means drinking at least 600 ml/1 pint/2½ cups cool clear water 10–15 minutes before the run. You needn't worry that you'll be caught short because the liquid won't have time to reach the kidneys before the start, and once exercise begins they slow down anyway. I've used this method of hydrating before marathons in the Far East, in high temperatures and high humidity, with great success.

Don't wait until race day to test my theory — experiment during training. If you've gauged your fluid intake correctly, your urine should be pale yellow. If it's dark orange you've allowed yourself to become dehydrated and no de-fizzed Coke, coffee or electrolyte drink would have prevented it.

RUNNING LIGHT

Dieting is big business and it thrives because the majority of us are searching for the soft option. Whether it's a pill, potion, powder, or high-protein, low-fat, high-fibre, low-calorie, diet — we're suckers for the latest craze. There's no doubt that each will spell instant success for someone, but if you don't see yourself living on papaya juice and powdered seaweed, there is an alternative.

Regular exercise combined with a balanced wholefood diet must be the thinking person's solution to weight control, but if you need a little extra help you might find the following tips useful.

1 Choose wholefoods — they will fill you up for longer because they're full of fibre.
2 Don't skip breakfast — eating it will push your calorie burning rate (BMR) into top gear.
3 If you're prone to nibbling, keep a bowl or bag of raw vegetables close at hand to dull the appetite.
4 Eat slowly. Experts say it takes roughly 20 minutes to feel full.
5 Cut out fatty meats and fried foods. Avoid hard cheeses and full-fat milk.
6 Don't even buy products containing sugar — that way you make the decision at the supermarket, not the kitchen cupboard.
7 Don't buy sliced bread. Cut your own thick slices, which will mean you'll only be eating one layer of butter or margarine instead of three or four.
8 Drink more water and restrict alcohol and fruit juices. It's far better to eat your fruit whole and benefit from the fibre as well as the juice.
9 Consider a vegetarian diet. Statistically, vegetarians tend to be leaner than carnivores, probably because they eat less fat and more fibre.
10 Schedule your run for before a main meal as running often acts as an appetite suppressant.
11 Many runners on high mileage eat five or six small meals a day which can be less fattening than three large meals.
12 Attempt to eat the majority of your calories before the evening. Eating late at night, when your BMR is winding down, will result in more calories stored as fat.

Remember, no single food is fattening — only if we consume more calories than we can use as energy do we gain weight. If you've been greedy with the calories one day, you'll have to run it off the next.

VITAL VITAMINS

You should be able to acquire all the vitamins you need from a balanced diet but, as we all know, runners don't always find time to take this aspect of fitness too seriously. If the majority of your calories come from convenience foods and sweets you should consider a good multivitamin.

Vitamins A, D, E and K are all fat soluble and can therefore be stored by the body. Vitamins B and C are water soluble which means we run a greater risk of deficiency as they can't be stored.

VITAMIN A — necessary for healthy eyes, skin and for fighting infection.
Source — dairy products, liver, carrots, green and yellow vegetables and fruit, egg yolk.

VITAMIN B_1 — essential for the nervous system, aids digestion and helps to convert carbohydrates into energy.
Source — brewer's yeast, wholewheat products, peanuts, pork, oatmeal, vegetables, offal (variety meats), milk, yeast extract, fish, soya beans, Brazil nuts, millet.

VITAMIN B_2 — helps cells to utilize oxygen for the release of energy and metabolism of carbohydrates.
Source — milk, offal (variety meats), eggs, green vegetables, poultry, dried yeast, fish, cheese, wheatgerm, almonds.

VITAMIN B_6 — healthy blood and enzyme reactions.
Source — milk, wheatgerm, blackstrap molasses, liver, kidney, heart, eggs, beef, cabbage, soya beans, brewer's yeast, walnuts, peanuts, corn, yeast extract.

VITAMIN B_{12} — healthy blood and nervous system.
Source — liver, eggs, cheese, milk, beef, pork, kidney, alfalfa.

VITAMIN C — increases resistance to infection and helps in the absorption of iron.

Source — citrus fruits, tomatoes, berries, melon, cabbage, red pepper, broccoli, kale, potatoes, parsley.

VITAMIN D — strong bones and teeth and helps calcium absorption.
Source — fish liver oils, dairy products and sunlight.

VITAMIN E — maintenance of cell membranes and helps to supply oxygen, producing greater endurance.
Source — wheatgerm, vegetable oils, nuts, legumes, soya beans, leafy green vegetables, whole grain cereals and eggs.

MAGNESIUM — helps to metabolise vitamin C and calcium and also in the conversion of blood sugar into energy.
Source — figs, nuts, seeds, apples, lemons, green vegetables.

CALCIUM — necessary for strong bones and teeth. Helps to metabolise iron, delays muscle fatigue, increases stamina and is thought to lower blood pressure and prevent cramps. Exercise increases its absorption.
Source — milk products, soya beans, sardines, salmon, sunflower seeds, dried beans, peanuts, walnuts, green vegetables, figs, almonds, watercress.

IRON — promotes growth, fights disease and fatigue, prevents anaemia, assists the transport of oxygen from the lungs to the muscles. It's the mineral most often found to be low in runners.
Source — beans, lean red meat, breakfast cereals, dried fruit, blackstrap molasses, liver, clams, oysters, millet.
   Vitamin C taken with iron greatly helps its absorption — eat fruit with meals and sprinkle lemon juice over salads.
   Use iron cookware and don't drink coffee any less than an hour before meals as caffeine hinders absorption of iron.

POTASSIUM — works with sodium to retain a balance of salts for nerve and muscle function.
Source — bananas, tomatoes, citrus fruits, dried fruit, green leafy vegetables, sunflower seeds, watercress, potatoes.

ZINC — helps brain function and bodily systems.
Source — red meat, wheatgerm, brewer's yeast, pumpkin seeds, eggs, mustard.

INDEX